Let's Go Home To Indiana Harbor

*Reflections From
Mid-Town America*

Let's Go Home To Indiana Harbor

*Reflections From
Mid-Town America*

By Warren G. Landrum, Jr.

Warland Books
Grand Prairie, Texas

Let's Go Home To Indiana Harbor

Published by:

Warland Books
2791 Explorador
Grand Prairie, TX 75054
Warrenglandrum@hotmail.com

Author photos (biography and back cover) by Carol Landrum
Cover basketball photo and photo on page 27
used with permission of Daryl Bridgeman

Warren Landrum, Publisher / Editorial Director
Yvonne Rose/Quality Press, Production Coordinator
The Printed Page, Cover & Text Layout

ALL RIGHTS RESERVED

No part of this book may be reproduced or transmitted in any form or by any means—electronic or mechanical, including photocopying, recording or by any information storage and retrieved system without written permission from the authors, except for the inclusion of brief quotations in a review.

The publication is designed to provide accurate and authoritative information in regard to the subject matter covered. It is sold with the understanding that the Publisher is not engaged in rendering legal or other professional services. If legal advice or other expert assistance is required, the services of a competent professional person should be sought. "All quotes used within this book are used pursuant to the Fair Use provision of the U.S. Copyright Law."

Warland Books are available at special discounts for bulk purchases, sales promotions, fund raising or educational purposes.

© Copyright 2009 by Warren Landrum and Warland Books
ISBN 13: 978-0-9787355-9-3 / ISBN 10: 0-9787355-9-5
Library of Congress Control Number: 2009920913

Dedication

This book is dedicated to those who have gone on before me to pave the way—my parents, Warren Sr. and Bynetta Landrum, and my brother Robert "Duke" Landrum.

Also, to my beloved wife Carol, daughter Suzette, and sister DeAngela "Dee" Barthe, who remain the three most important women in my life.

Finally, I'd like to dedicate this book to Louise Jackson, aka 'Ms. Jackson', who is the 'Last of the Mohicans'.

Acknowledgements

I would like to acknowledge first and foremost, Kenny Davis (ECW, class of '85) for creating the website, ECW Online. Reading some of the comments posted by my fellow ECW Senators on that site is what inspired me to write this book. By doing so, my intent is to share with a much larger audience, hopefully, an idea of what it was like to grow up in such a wonderfully diverse, multi-cultural environment as we did while growing up in Indiana Harbor in East Chicago, Indiana. That era, from the 1960's through the 1980's was also a special time in The Harbor, and in America, as a whole, I believe. If we can recapture some of that 'magic' and send it back out into today's world, I believe that everyone it touches will be enriched.

Just as important as Kenny was in creating the website, are all those who contributed their memories. As I write this Acknowledgement, there are almost 1300 members on the site. To those whose remembrances I used, I say a special thanks. And to those who I didn't use, I say thank you as well, for taking a minute to take a trip back down Memory Lane. It was extraordinary to see so many names and faces that I know from my high school days.

We ARE the Senators!!!!

Contents

Dedication. v

Acknowledgements. vi

I Wonder ix

Prologue xi

Chapter 1. Brief History of East Chicago 1
    What Was Going On. 3

Chapter 2. Fern Street 4

Chapter 3. Carey Street, Block and Pennsy (on the block) . 11
    Carey Street 13
    Pennsylvania Avenue. 16
    What Was Going On 20

Chapter 4. The Melting Pot 21

Chapter 5. Growing up in The Harbor— Prelude 33
    What Was Going On 35

Chapter 6. Growing up in The Harbor 36
    Warren Remembers. 36

Chapter 7. Growing Up in The Harbor 43
    ECW Senators Remember 43

Chapter 8. Youngstown Sheet & Tube 60
    What Was Going On 62

Chapter 9. The Mills 63

Chapter 10. Washington Park and Block Stadium 69
    Washington Park 69
    Block Stadium 75

Chapter 11. The Tunnel and The Bridge 78
    What Was Going On 83

Chapter 12. The Lake 84
    The Lake (As I See It) 84

Chapter 13. Basketball Revisited 90
    What Was Going On 96

Chapter 14. The Last Chapter 97

Epilogue 101

Bonus Chapter 103
    The Midnight Fishing Trip 103

In Conclusion 108

Appendix A 109

Appendix B 110

References 113

About the Author.... 115

Order Form 117

I Wonder

5/17/01

Will Anybody care when I pass away
Will anyone cry or shed a Tear for Me on that day
And I wonder what on Earth
My Heavenly Ledger Book will say
Did I make a Difference in any Life
In any Way?
Did I lift Somebody up
Did I make Somebody smile
Did I spread a little Sunshine
As I walked along Life's Miles
If not, it's not too late, I hope
I can start—right now—Today
To make a Difference
So that the World will know
I passed along This Way

Let's Go Home to Indiana Harbor

Prologue

The year 2008 ended as a most momentous, historic, defining moment in the course of United States history. On Tuesday, November 4th, 2008, a 47-year old man of African-American heritage, Barack Hussein Obama, was elected as 44th President of the United States of America—the first African-American President, instantly becoming the most powerful man in the world. But what makes this moment and this man even more unique is that Barack Obama is truly a man of the world. Although classified as African-American, as everyone knows by now, he is the offspring of a Kenyan father and a European-American woman from Kansas. He grew up in Indonesia and Hawaii and was raised by his European-American grandparents in Hawaii. So Barack Obama is truly a "Citizen of the World".

And that brings us to this book. It seems as though all the stars are aligning and the pages that follow on this book are a story that was begging to be told—right now! The vision that Barack Obama has for a unified America of One Nation, One People, regardless of political inclination, race, religion, or color is actually the America I grew up in, in East Chicago, Indiana in a section of town affectionately known as "The

Harbor". In our town at that time, just about all the kids had either a Dad or an Uncle or a cousin or *somebody* who worked in one of the local steel mills, whether it was Inland Steel or Youngstown Sheet and Tube in East Chicago, or over at "The Big Mill"—US Steel, in Gary. So we were all in the same boat. And what a mixed up lot we were. We had Mexicans, and Poles, and Blacks, and Serbians, and Czechs, and Romanians, and Puerto Ricans, and Jews, and Episcopalians, and Catholics, and Baptists, and Methodists, and probably some more nationalities and religions that I can't even think of or remember. We truly earned our nickname of "The Melting Pot" that I remember seeing our area called on a few different occasions in a few different stories.

I remember often telling my wife of twenty years, Carol, how it was so cool growing up like that in a place where we really did not experience any real prejudice. I think that the first time I experienced any overt prejudice or racism was when I first went away to college down in West Lafayette, Indiana to attend Purdue University. I don't know if people down there looked down on me because I was from "Da Region", which is what the rest of Indiana called the Northwest corner of the state that included Gary, East Chicago and Hammond or because I was Black. I also don't think it was mostly or just the people from West Lafayette. I think that in encountering a lot of the White kids from different parts of the United States, that's where I felt the most sting of prejudice in their remarks, either directly to me, or to each other, about me and my friends.

But anyway, back to why the time is right for this book to happen now. As it happens, a guy from my High School, the East Chicago Washington (ECW) Senators, started a website

Prologue

this summer for anyone who had ever attended, worked at, or taught at ECW. By the time my sister told me about this site in mid-August and I joined, I was the 681st member. As I write this, about twelve weeks later, the membership count is at 1279—an increase of 598, as word continues to get out about the site. The site creator allowed for Forums and Groups to be created by the members and besides re-connecting with old friends, in reading through some of these forums, it makes me realize that my other fellow Senators also realize what a special time and especially what a special place we grew up in when we were all truly one. The remembrances and recollections posted by my fellow Senators came from some who graduated as far back as in the late 1950's all the way up to the mid-1980's when they shut the doors on our beloved ECW for the last time.

I want to make it clear right now, though, that The Harbor was no utopia. We had our share of crime, and bullies, just like any other city. And we also had gangs, and corrupt politicians and cops, and air pollution from the mill. But it's not the purpose of this book to dwell on the negative or to try and document everything that was going on around town while I was growing up. I simply want to focus on the positive to give people some good memories to look back upon—nothing more, nothing less.

I have written this book so that it can be read either sequentially or so that you can just go directly to a chapter of your choice from the Table of Contents, and read that chapter in isolation, without losing any of the meaning, or overall 'mood' of the book.

I've also included little one page tidbits called "What's Going On" throughout the book. These pages tell what the

Oscar-winning movie was that year, which television shows got the Emmy awards for Best Comedy and Best Drama, and what the Grammy-winning Record of the Year and R&B Record of the Year were. Each of these pages covers a 5-year period, (ie 1960—1964) so that it may spur your memory as to what you were going through when that song or movie or TV show came out.

So I want to share some of their stories and remembrances, as well as some of the recollections they have rekindled in me of some of the pre-high school years in the Harbor, because a reflection of ECW and The Harbor is really a reflection on the core values that America was founded on and a reflection on how people could live together if the principles of the US Constitution and of The Pledge of Allegiance—"…one nation, under God, indivisible, with Liberty and Justice for All…" were truly a reality.

Chapter 1

Brief History of East Chicago

To really understand how The Harbor fits into East Chicago geographically and culturally, to some degree, it is going to be necessary to first give a brief history of the city. So here we go.

The City of East Chicago was founded in 1888 and incorporated in 1893. It was originally known as the Twin City, with East Chicago (western section) separated from Indiana Harbor (aka The Harbor) by a vast rail yard that served as the gateway to get steel to Chicago and out west. (*A Rich History, n.d.*). An overpass on Columbus Drive (The Viaduct) was built in the early 1930's and that helped to connect the two main parts of the city together. All of the steel mills in East Chicago were in The Harbor, situated along the southern tip of Lake Michigan. There were other steel mills along this curve in Lake Michigan, stretching from the south side of Chicago, all the way to Portage, Indiana, about 40 or 50 miles to the east.

Most of the early immigrants to East Chicago came from Eastern European countries, including Czechoslovakia, Serbia, Romania and Poland. Thus, you had a lot of names ending in "ich" or "ic" or "ski". Most of these immigrants came to pursue 'The American Dream" and better lives for themselves and their children. But the thing that helped to enrich East Chicago was that most of these immigrants kept their own cultures through their churches and other organizations. I can still look back and remember all of the beautiful Eastern European or Gothic style churches that were spread out throughout The Harbor at the time I was growing up. I knew they were pretty then, but it was only when I got to visit Europe as an adult, that I saw the distinctly European influence under which these edifices were constructed.

Due to the two World Wars and a succession of labor strikes, East Chicago and The Harbor became even more diverse, as African-Americans (or Negroes as they were called during that time) came from the South in droves to fill the manufacturing jobs that the steel mills offered. There were also a lot of Hispanics from Mexico and Puerto Rico who found their way up North, to add to this smorgasbord of ethnicities, and to help create the final mix that became The Harbor. (*A Rich History, n.d.*). The Harbor was definitely more diverse than the East Chicago part of the city, primarily due to the proximity of those homes and living quarters to the mills.

That is a very brief synopsis of the early history of the shaping of East Chicago and The Harbor. It is brief, but it is necessary to understand some of the topics discussed later on in this book.

So let's get right to some of them, shall we? Let's start with taking a closer look at what was happening on some of the streets in some of the neighborhoods, as viewed through the author's eyes and the eyes of my fellow Senators as we travel back in time to another era, a simpler era… Do you wanna go? C'mon… let's do it!

What Was Going On

1960—1964

Year	Top Song Grammies —Record of the Year, Artist —R & B Song of the Year, Artist	
1960	Mack the Knife	Bobby Darin
	What a Diff'rence a Day Makes	Dinah Washington
1961	Theme From A Summer Place	Percy Faith
	Let The Good Times Roll	Ray Charles
1962	Moon River	Henry Mancini
	Hit The Road Jack	Ray Charles
1963	I Left My Heart in San Francisco	Tony Bennett
	I Can't Stop Loving You	Ray Charles
1964	Days of Wine and Roses	Henry Mancini
	Busted	Ray Charles

Year	Oscar-Winning Movie	Other Movies
1960	The Apartment	Psycho
1961	West Side Story	The Hustler
1962	Lawrence of Arabia	To Kill a Mockingbird
1963	Tom Jones	Lilies of The Field
1964	My Fair Lady	Mary Poppins

Year	TV Drama Emmy	TV Comedy Emmy
1960	Playhouse 90	Art Carney Special
1961	Macbeth, Hallmark Hall of Fame	The Jack Benny Show
1962	The Defenders	The Bob Newhart Show
1963	The Defenders	The Dick Van Dyke Show
1964	The Defenders	The Dick Van Dyke Show

Chapter 2

Fern Street

It all began on the Street. Or more specifically, on MY street—Fern Street. Or even MORE specifically, in the lower half of the 3900 block of Fern Street. Yeah, there were other streets around town—streets like Carey Street and Pennsylvania Avenue, but for me, Fern Street is the root and base of where my childhood memories begin. When I was born, we lived on Canal Port, over in Nu-Addition, and then moved over to Deodar Street by the time I started 2nd grade, but when we moved into 3906 Fern Street in 1963, that's when the beginning of the rest of my life really started.

Fern Street was laid out with about fifteen houses on each side of the street, with the buildings on both ends of the side of the street across from our house, being brick apartment duplexes. These houses were all built back in the 1920's, I think, and they were built mostly for the families who worked in the Steel Mills.

East Chicago, Indiana, along with Gary, was a Steel Mill town, and housed two of the major steel mills that ran along the southern tip of Lake Michigan, stretching from the south side of Chicago, to Michigan City, about 40 or 50 miles away. We had Youngstown Sheet and Tube Company, and Inland Steel

Company. They, along with 'The Big Mill" aka Bethlehem Steel over in Gary, produced most of the steel coming out of "Da Region" as the Northwest corner of Indiana was called, and also probably employed the vast majority of people in the area. I did not know anyone growing up, who did not have a parent or uncle or cousin or someone, working in the mills. East Chicago, or at least the side of town that I lived on, was also known as Indian Harbor, or more affectionately, "The Harbor". It was called that because when all the ships came in from Lake Michigan to either pick up steel product or drop off raw materials, they would come into the harbor that led to the various steel mills.

Anyway, back to Fern Street. Our house at 3906 Fern Street was not particularly big. I'm guessing it probably ran about 1000 to 1200 square feet, if that. But it seemed plenty big enough to a 9-year old, which is what I was at the time we moved in. It had a back yard, where we could play, and a couple cherry trees, and a pear tree, which we could climb, and a garage that, from its roof, we could use as a base to hop on our neighbor, Miss Hazel's garage roof, and get into her apple tree to pick some of those juicy little green apples!

I even somehow remember the day we moved in. It was a Sunday, and my Uncle Porter—my Dad's brother, who was my favorite uncle, helped with the moving. Uncle Porter liked to imbibe in the spirits and he worked in the steel mills, along with my Dad, and my Uncle Havon; but I remember him as a big gentle Teddy Bear of a man, who always had a kind word for me and would always take the time to play with me whenever he came over to visit. I remember Uncle Porter used to always call me "Yoshto", whatever the heck that meant. I was also told later in life that I was a lot like

Uncle Porter, because I could sing, and because I had such an easy-going demeanor. Uncle Porter, apparently used to sing around the region in a Gospel Quartet, and they were really good from what I was told. I was also told that Uncle Porter was quite the ladies' man!

But getting back to Fern Street—as I said, the lower half of the 3900 block of Fern Street was the core of my world back in those days. Within the first seven houses on the other side of the block, and our house on our side, was where most of my first, best friends came from. You had The Hintons at 3903 with Ricky, and later Phillip and Timmy; The Riveras at 3905 with Johnnie, Jose, Gloria and Margie; The Lopez's at 3909 with Johnny, Louie, Christine, Teresa and Nita; The Kleckas at 3913 with Bobby, Rachel and Little Florrie; and us, The Landrums, at 3906, with me and my little brat sister, Dee. We had my brother Duke, too, but Duke had polio and was afflicted with mental retardation, so unfortunately, he could not get out and play with us. Later on, when they moved into 3912, we had The Abrams kids, too—and there was a bunch of them. So that was the gang. As you can see from the names, we had Mexican kids, Black kids, and Polish kids playing together right there at a young age. That's how it was all over The Harbor and that's how our town got its nickname as "The Melting Pot". We'll get into that more in a later chapter.

Anyway, we would play kickball and dodge ball in the streets together, play hide-and-seek in and around and through each other's yards and alley-ways, play strike-out against the wall behind Joe Gray's corner store, and play baseball in my back yard. I still can't believe how we could have a field with all 4 bases in a yard that small, where the outfield and home run barrier was our garage, which had to have been all of 30 or 40 feet from home plate! Boy, we must have been awfully small—or awfully weak hitters—back then.

When we were not outside raising some kind of childish hell, we would be in somebody's house, more than likely eating. The Lopez's had the best tamales in the world! Or we'd be having fried chicken or bar-b-q at my house, or maybe hot dogs at The Hintons. One thing we knew was that we would never have to worry about being hungry as long as SOMEBODY on our half-block had food. I'm not saying that to suggest we were poor or anything, it's just that whoever's house or yard we'd be playing at when it was dinner time, was most likely where we'd have a bite to eat too. Sometimes when I got back to my own house, I wouldn't even be hungry for our OWN dinner. But I'd eat it anyway because my mother was the best cook in the world. As I look back, I don't see how I, or any of us, got out of that neighborhood without weighing at least 300 pounds!!

Thinking back on it, another amazing thing that the lower half of the 3900 block of Fern Street had was The Club. This club was a real example of how East Chicago and The Harbor, in particular, was a real melting pot. The Club was started by Mr. John Brozovic. Mr. Brozovic, at that time, was a White Man, probably in about his mid-to-late 50's and he formed this club with a small group of Black, Mexican, and Polish kids back in the early 1960's. He lived in that big red-brick duplex apartment building at 3901 Fern Street. He lived there with his sister Jean, who was also a kind old white woman, and his sister-in-law, Martha, who we thought at that time must have been kin to the Wicked Witch of the West. She was a mean old woman!

But anyhow, I know that Mr. Brozovic was some kind of 'big shot' on the political scene back then, but I could not remember exactly what he was. So I just 'googled' 'John Brozovic' and an article was returned from the July 1961 archive edition of The Hammond Times, our main local newspaper at the time, that mentioned him as the North Township Trustee. So I guess that's what he was. But when I think back on it, I can't imagine too many other cities or towns in America in which something like this would have happened. Mr. Brozovic had even created a secret handshake for us, that we had to give him whenever we ran up to meet him and greet him when we'd see him after school. We'd run up to him, give him the secret handshake, and most of the time, right after that, our grubby little hands would be filled with change! I think that's one of the main things we liked about Mr. Brozovic and The Club!! Also, whenever Mr. Stigger, the Ice-Cream Man, would drive down the street in his Ice-Cream Truck, if Mr. Brozovic was around, we knew there'd be free ice-cream for all.

I called my sister in Atlanta a couple days ago to see if she remembered there being a secret handshake, so I could make sure I was not hallucinating , and sure enough, she confirmed it. She even gave me another Mr. Brozovic story. She said that on one occasion, she and our Dad were down on Columbus Drive watching a parade. She said that one of the parade cars started coming in their direction, and it had Mr. Brozovic in it, smiling and waving to people. She said that when he spotted her, he had her come on up into the cars and she finished the parade riding in the car with him. She said that she would never forget that!

We did more on Fern Street than just run up and down the street playing with each other. Fern Street had a true sense of community, and everybody on the street watched out for each other. This WAS a common thing in our town and in other towns around America at that time, as I have since learned. I know just about anybody I talk to that grew up back in the 60's and 70's will tell a story about how, if they messed up and did something bad or wrong, one of their adult neighbors would chastise or punish them about it; and then by the time they reached home, word would have already gotten there, and they'd REALLY catch it at home. I know for us, the main neighbor like this was Miss Hazel, who lived right next door to us. Miss Hazel MUST have been in her 70's or so when we were kids, and she was around giving us grief for at least the next decade or so until at least the time I graduated from high school and left home. But, God Bless her soul, I don't know what we would have done or how we would have turned out without Miss Hazel or Miss Abrams, who lived another few houses down, or Mr. Bailey, or any of the rest of them who watched out for us and kept us in line.

We also pitched in to help each other in times of trouble or natural disaster. I remember when The Big Snow of 1967 came. That was one of the biggest snowstorms of the century. It closed down the schools and the whole city, really. I remember my Uncle Havon could not get back to his home in Hammond, during the snowstorm, and afterwards because of all the snow in the streets and the drifts that had buried a lot of cars. So he wound up staying with us for what seemed like weeks, but I'm sure now was only days. I remember all the stores had run out of milk and bread, so if you had not stocked up on these before the storm hit, you were out of luck. We would have to help each other dig our cars out so that people could try to go to work, and we'd have to even help each other dig paths from the porches down to the sidewalks, just so we could get to the cars. My sister reminded me that my Dad had to help Mr. Hinton across the street dig his car out so he could get Miss Verlie to the hospital to deliver Little Timmy. So we will always remember the year Timmy Hinton was born!

So that was a sample of some of the things that were happening on the street I grew up on from age 8 until I left high school for college. Now I want to take you 'cross-town' in The Harbor to talk about life on some of the other streets in town. **Let's Go !!!**

Chapter 3

Carey Street, Block and Pennsy (on the block)

Obviously there were more streets in The Harbor besides Fern Street. As in all cities (I would imagine), you have the so-called 'right' and 'wrong' side of the tracks—parts of town where you just didn't venture if you knew what was good for you. Well, maybe Mayberry did not have such locales, but The Harbor sure did—or so I thought as I was growing up.

But I was kind of hard-headed, young, and naïve enough not to know better, so when my best friend moved 'cross town to one of those streets, Carey Street, I didn't give a second thought to walking or riding my bike over to his house after school or on weekends, mostly so we could hook up and play basketball somewhere. I guess I figured as long as I had George with me, I was safe, and no one would mess with me, the 'Outsider' from 'cross town. And no one ever did.

But Block and Pennsy was a different story. Those two streets—Block Avenue and Pennsylvania Avenue, literally WERE across the tracks. If you went down Guthrie Street, the 'main' entrance into that part of town was right across from The Big Building and Lincoln Food Fair—crossing the tracks on a street that led into what was probably the middle of that neighborhood. I think I may have gone across those tracks, maybe once or twice in all the time I lived in The Harbor. It was just where the poor, rough, tough, ghetto people were supposed to live, and I was not told any different in all my time there.

But it's amazing how living life, and maturity, and the passage of time, and knowledge and experience can change one's views on perceived realities. After I first went away to college and started returning to The Harbor, from time to time, I'd start venturing over to Carey Street more and more as my circle of friends and acquaintances came to include kids who lived on those blocks. I started seeing that they really were not that much different from me, and as I stated in the introduction, pretty much ALL of us had someone related to us working in the steel mills, so we were all pretty much in the same boat whether we knew it or not ! As I also stated in the introduction to this book, a guy from my high school started an online website for anyone who had ever attended, worked at, or taught at East Chicago Washington (ECW), which was the high school in The Harbor. He allowed visitors to this site (all ECW Senators) to create Forums to talk about remembrances they had on any subject from their high school years. As it happened, a couple people from Carey Street and from Pennsylvania Avenue started forums. In reading through some of the postings in these forums, it made me finally realize that these guys shared some of the same beliefs and went through some of the same things I did growing up. It also made me realize that those residents had their own sense of community, just as those of us from Fern Street did. Some of the memories were so poignant and revealing that I felt I HAD to dedicate a chapter in this book to recounting them, as this would also give a better picture of what it was like to grow up in The Harbor. So let's start with Carey Street...

Carey Street

"Carey Street had a vibe all of its own... You had to live there to understand it... or at least nearby like Drummond..."

Diane Jones Dillard, August 15, 2008
1959—1965

... but for some reason my friends on Drummond could not come on Carey Street to my house because Carey was "too rough" according to their parents ...maybe it depended on what era you were in, but way back in the day there was that sentiment among some out there... But Carey did have the pool room, the tree people, kin folks, and the Grimm Bros. fighting in the middle of the street, throwin' bricks at each other... so maybe a little rougher around the edges, but it was "all good"

Diane Jones Dillard, September 18, 2008
1959 - 1965

ALL RIGHT CAREY STREETERS!!!!!!!. We had the best people in the world. I most remember how everyone watched after everyone else's children. If they had something to eat, so did you. The street looked much bigger to me growing up. The corner was busy all the time!!!

Toni Walker, August 16, 2008
1969 - 1973

I know that's right. My cousins and friends and I have laughed about how many people lived in one block! We were in the 3900 block, and it seemed like hundreds of people lived there, but one thing about it, everybody knew everybody, and for the most part looked out for each other. And anybody's mama would check you if you did wrong. The 'corner' had a life of its own, our uncle made sure we didn't even slow down at the corner.

Diane Jones Dillard, August 16, 2008
1959 - 1965

Hey Neighbors,

Carey Street Day was wonderful. Yes, I remember the love and support we had for each other, and it is still there. So many great memories. I am on Carey Street at least once a week. My mother still lives there, 3900 block, and I see many of my friends still standing and sitting around talking about who knows what. Remember Davis and Burts grocery stores? They helped many of us make it through the day. I will inform others about the Carey Streeters. God Bless.

Elozia Ann Jernigan-Neeley, August 17, 2008
1964 - 1969

I lived on the 38th block. We all played together and were really tight. Everyone was family and supported each other. I remember playing neighborhood baseball, football and tag games.

Sandra Kemp, August 18, 2008
1972 - 1975

Good old Carey Street. When you are born and raised at the same address until after graduating from ECW, that street is in your blood. I went to the last Carey Street picnic and the rain dampened it a little, but as soon as the rain left, the people went right on like nothing happened. I wish to commend the ones in charge of this event each and every year. They do a wonderful job, because people come from far and near to just be in the midst of the Carey street vibes. Those Carey street days are gone but will never be forgotten. My brother Lonnie is deceased, Ronnie in Detroit, MI, sisters, Elozia in Gary, IN, Shirley in East Chicago, and I am still in East Chicago.

Annetta (Jernigan) Copeland
(old address-3929 Carey Street)
Annetta (Jernigan) Copeland, August 26, 2008
1966 - 1969

Hey fellow Carey Streeters, we were really living back then, we just didn't know it. We might not have had the best of everything, but we definitely had everything we needed. I can remember Ralph Smith, Larry Williams, Lester Johnson, Robert Brown, and whoever else, were always at our house. We played cards, listened to music, and watched television. Sometimes we just sat around the kitchen table and talked. My mom was a single parent and didn't mind the guys coming over because they knew how to conduct themselves, without a doubt.

Frankie Askew Banks, August 29, 2008
1963 - 1969

Wasn't it something, doors unlocked… could stay up until all hours of the night and not be scared… Everybody watched out for one another……

ONE BIG HAPPY FAMILY !!!

Nettie (Person) Collins, September 10, 2008
1963—1968

I had to laugh when you said "where is the watermelon man now" :) That was something now that I really think about it… Street vendors coming down the street selling *everything you needed on a daily basis it seemed... Wouldn't that be convenient now??? Think of the gas, and time we could save... They really were "the good old days"! Does anyone remember Miss Young, she had a garden in her front yard, and if you accidentally threw a ball in there... Forget it! She wouldn't let you get it back, if you tried, she'd chase you out her yard.*

Diane Jones Dillard, September 16, 2008
1959 - 1965

So those are some remembrances and a little taste of what it was like on the Carey Street side of town back in the day. Now let's move across town to Block and Pennsy and see what those folks have to say...

Pennsylvania Avenue

The good old days on Pennsylvania Street...I remember Mrs. Haynes always watching us from her window and telling everything we said and did... Mr. Haynes candy store next door to our house... During those years, we were able to walk the streets and be safe because everybody was basically close friends. I remember walking to church with my grandfather Samuel Perdue, along with Poochie, Brian, and Billy. I think Robin and Marlon was also with us... We was at Faith Temple C.O.G.I.C. all day long... I remember the little church across the street where my grandmother Willie Perdue and I would attend... Wow! I am so happy to have fond memories of Pennsylvania Street where I can share them with my children... The good old days... Yes!

Posted by Karen Lynn George-Dates, August 15, 2008
1974—1978

I know that's right girlfriend, if it wasn't for Penn. St. we wouldn't be the women we are today. That street taught us how to deal or no deal. Just keepin' it all the way real.
                                Kim S. Askew, August 20, 2008
                                               1984 - 1986

I spent every summer at Penn Center the best place in town. Don't even talk about waiting on the bus to take us skating every Saturday night!!!! Plus the buses that took us to Old Chicago, White Sox Park, the Zoo, and Six Flags just to name a few. Yes!!! I was there for it all.
                                Terrilyn Lloyd, September 2, 2008
                                                1980 - 1981

I grew up at 3800 block of Block and Pennsylvania from 1947 to 1960 or 61. At that time, both streets went all the way to Baby Park. St Luke's Church (I think now it is down by Field School) was on the corner of Pennsylvania, and Tabernacle (which is now on Butternut) was at about the middle of the block. There was also St. Jude's Catholic Church a little further up the street. Next to the Catholic church, you could go over to Block street. There was a Catholic school that was used as an Annex to Field School for some years in the 50's. When we were kids, we played a many night in the streets and around the school. When I grew up everybody on those streets was family. Yes, them old biddys (smile) did see everything and told everything, but they were trying to keep us out of trouble (I realize that now, I'm really getting old (smile)
                                Helen Smith Flynn, September 16, 2008
                                                1956—1961

I feel kind of bad for the families on Pennsy now. They don't have the love that we had for each other. You could go to a friend's house and play, and if you got out of line their mom would spank you and send you home for your mom to beat the crap out of you. Nowadays, if you look at a kid doing wrong, their mother wants to jump on you. I never thought I would miss growing up on Pennsy and Block.

Lynn Threatt, September 9, 2008
1979—1983

We were the closest group of family and friends anywhere. Our moms all got along. They shared food, hardships, and laughter. I remember sleeping outside on lawn chairs while everyone sat in front of their doors talking and laughing all night. We played together, laughed together, and cried together. I remember when we were going to the first grade, my momma took all the kids to Penn. Center so we could get our shots. Me and Magaly broke and ran all around that center trying to get away from those needles. Man… Pennsylvania will always hold fond memories in my heart.

Roshanta Buggs, September 15, 2008
1984 - 1986

I WAS BORN AND RAISED THERE AND THAT WAS THE BEST BLOCK IN THE WORLD. THANK YOU EAST CHICAGO FOR MAKIN' ME THE WOMAN I AM TODAY!

Magaly Gonzalez-Williams, August 4, 2008
1984 - 1986

FOR SURE… THIS WAS THE STREET THAT MADE ALL OF US WHO WE ARE. THEY USED TO THINK NOTHING GOOD COULD COME FROM THAT SIDE OF THE TRACKS, BUT THAT'S A LIE. WE WERE ALL

CLOSE AND WE WERE A REAL NEIGHBORHOOD… SOMETHING THAT IS MISSING THESE DAYS. I WOULD NOT HAVE TRADED THOSE DAYS FOR THE WORLD….MUCH LOVE…..B

Baron Moss, September 23, 2008
1983 - 1986

So there it is. We weren't so different after all—those of us on Fern Street and Carey Street and Pennsylvania Avenue. We ALL had that sense of community and we all looked out for each other in our own little worlds and streets. I've got a feeling it was like that on EVERY street in The Harbor. As I said before, we all were basically in the same boat, what with just about everyone's Dad or Uncle or Mama or Sister or Brother or Cousin or SOMEBODY working in the Mills. That's why we really did not experience any racism or real prejudice in The Harbor for the most part. Now if you went over to Honky Town, which was over in what we called East Chicago, that was a different story. But the next chapter speaks a little to ECW students' memories of growing up in this wonderful melting pot… without racism and prejudice.

What Was Going On

1965—1969

Year	Top Song Grammies - Record of the Year, Artist - R & B Song of the Year, Artist	
1965	The Girl From Ipanema	Stan Getz
	How Glad I Am	Nancy Wilson
1966	A Taste of Honey	Herb Alpert
	Papa's Got a Brand New Bag	James Brown
1967	Strangers in the Night	Frank Sinatra
	Crying Time	Ray Charles
1968	Up, Up and Away	The Fifth Dimension
	Respect	Aretha Franklin
1969	Mrs. Robinson	Simon and Garfunkel
	Sitting on the Dock of the Bay	Otis Redding

Year	Oscar-Winning Movie	Other Movies
1965	The Sound of Music	Doctor Zhivago
1966	A Man for All Seasons	Who's Afraid of Virginia Woolf?
1967	In the Heat of the Night	Bonnie and Clyde
1968	Oliver	2001: A Space Odyssey
1969	Midnight Cowboy	Butch Cassidy and the Sundance Kid

Year	TV Drama Emmy	TV Comedy Emmy
1965		The Dick Van Dyke Show
1966	The Fugitive	The Dick Van Dyke Show
1967	Mission: Impossible	The Monkees
1968	Mission: Impossible	Get Smart
1969	NET Playhouse	Get Smart

Chapter 4

The Melting Pot

> "One of the not spoken enough strengths of growing up in East Chicago was that we blacks, whites, and Latinos got along, grew up, had fun and learned together. You just don't see enough of that anymore wherever I go in this country. I'm reminded of that here. Many of us just didn't care much about that kind of racial crap and strife back in the day, and it's something that I take with me and try to teach to my son and to my students.
>
> So for all of you who I've known over the years, thank you. It's a gift that's tough to repay and something that I appreciate more and more as the years pass".
> Dr. Christopher Mobley, Professor of Political Science
Chattanooga State Technical Community College
June 26, 2008
1974 - 1978

The following are some of the responses from the Forum to Dr. Chris Mobley, who grew up on Evergreen Street, about half-a-block over from my house, which was on Fern Street. As you can see, we all were enriched by the experience we had of growing up in a world with little or no prejudice.

I can't agree more Professor Mobley. I worked in Chicago for more than 25 years: WBEZ Radio, Illinois Institute of Technology, and FedEx. My co-workers would look at my yearbook and be amazed by the diversity of ECW. My white co-workers usually were the majority or more at their schools, same for my Latino & African-American co-workers. How did you get along with "Them"? Were there a lot of fights? I've said on this site and the Yahoo site that EC has made me capable of dealing with anyone in the workplace or any social occasion. I would "NEVER" trade my experience in The Harbor at The DUB for anything. Tim Clark(CUB Fan), Edwin Medina(CUB fan), Jaime Flores, Brent Givens, Tina Hanzi, Denise Melendez Torres, Doug Abernathy, Bobby Couch, William Mitchell, on and on. These people I have learned from, grown up with, and helped me become who I am. To all the members of this site, you have proven that color doesn't matter, keep letting the world know that. It's amazing what a tough little Steel Town can teach a big city and a country. Now if they'd just listen. I'm proud of you all Senators. I'm proud to be a Senator!!!!

Joel Moore, June 26, 2008
1976 - 1979

You are so right. I have lived in Indy for the last 14 years. I have seen a lot of changes culturally here over the years. There are a lot more Hispanics that have come to live here. People would say, "We don't want them here". I would tell them how I grew up and how East Chicago was. They couldn't understand it. Most had never been around Blacks, Mexicans, and Puerto Ricans until they were in college or the workplace. Where else could you go from house to house with your "friends" and experience different cultures without leaving your neighborhood? Black cultures, Mexican, Greek, Puerto Rican, Polish, Serbian, German. The list goes on and on. You just don't have those things anymore. I brought my wife and kids to E.C. to experience real Mexican food. Not Taco Bell. I wouldn't change anything about the way I grew up and the friends I made growing up in E.C. If cultures got along the way we did growing up the country would be a better place.

Anthony Mobley, June 26, 2008
1977 - 1981

Chris,

Boy did you hit on something! We instinctively knew about diversity before it became a commodity.

Living in Washington, DC, I have neighbors and friends from all over the world. When I stop and think about it, EC prepared me for dealing with different cultures, viewpoints and ways of life, so I did not have the extreme culture shock many people get when they come here to live. Diversity was just part of the fabric of the Harbor and we are richer people as a result.

I am not saying that everything was rosy, but generally speaking, we all got along. Like the saying goes, "we came over on different boats, but now we are all in the same boat."

I think one of the funniest things that I can share in this regard is the shock on people's faces here in DC when I say wicked things to them in Spanish AND Serbian!

Paree Roper, June 27, 2008
1972 - 1976

You all hit it on the head. In our neighborhood in just one block you could go to a German, Serbian, Polish, Mexican or Puerto Rican house and eat dinner and we did too.

It was so rich an environment to grow up in and I honestly can't recall any kind of racial tension other than that we would see on TV. There wasn't any in E.C. And I bet everyone from E.C. can say they had a best friend that was of another Race.

And Paree, you were right. Diversity was the order of the Day in E.C. and anyone who grew up there can go anywhere on the Planet and fit in. It is harder for E.C. people to wrap their mind around all the racial fuss because it was not fomented nor tolerated where we grew up. Proud to be from E.C. and the 'DUB'.

Greg "Chico" Davis, June 28, 2008
1969 - 1973

You know I grew up on the 39th block of Carey St. until I was 12. My family and our cousins were the last white families to live there. I grew up with the Johnson family, the Buggs family, and many more families that invited us into their homes for a bite to eat or a night to sleep. You're right on about us that grew up in the Harbor. We were color blind to race. We just lived our lives the way our Parents had put it into our Heart. I'm 57 now and my kids won't tolerate anyone, and I mean anyone, to talk that racial crap.

God bless you and your family and keep the faith. Who knows - maybe someone from the Harbor will be President one day and we all can live in harmony again,

James Merrill Pearcey, June 29, 2008
1963—1968

This place that we all still call home, no matter how far you go is blessed because of all the races that not only get along, but live as one. I have been blessed in having such a variety of friends and family, that it has enriched my life to an unspeakable measure. Words come short with what I'm trying to convey. Let me just put it this way. I was taught not to look at a person's color, race or nationality, but at their hearts. I really believe East Chicago was a melting pot for others that were taught in the same manner. We're all God's children.

Elizabeth Santos Quinones, June 30, 2008
1979 - 1983

Chris. East Chicago was a great place to learn about people. When I was at Franklin School, Block and Washington, my friends were from all races and backgrounds. We were able to be friends and the race stuff was never really the important issue. Many of my best memories are about going to people's houses, eating at their tables, sleeping over and throwing great birthday parties. I learned that it wasn't their color or the race, but the heart and soul of the person that made them special. I mean, we had a few fights, but that was rare. My best friends in school were Mexicans, Puerto Ricans, Spaniards, Blacks, Greeks, Serbians, Asians, Whites and too many others to remember. It really didn't matter - all kinds of people with different backgrounds and religions. Their families came to the region to work and raise their families, and to have a better life than they had somewhere else. As we got older, there was more of the us vs. them mentality. Now that we are older, I see so many prejudices. I try to look inside the person first. If they have good character, it doesn't matter where they came from. This is one of the best things I learned in school. The Harbor was my home. I was a Senator (still am). That reminds me, I need to tell my boys more about what it was like growing up in the Harbor... We need to pass this on to the next generation.

PS. This is a great country.

Marc Glick, July 3, 2008
1974 - 1978

I feel like this is a good place to insert the poem I wrote about East Chicago, that was in my book, "The Heart & Soul of a Black Man", that was published in October, 2006. The poem was entitled East Chicago, and it's funny, but Elizabeth uses almost the same words and phraseology as I used in my poem, when she describes East Chicago in the post right above this one. There MUST be some kind of connection there—the ECW, Harbor connection ☺ !

East Chicago

East Chicago, not Chicago
Is the place that I call Home
It's the place where my Roots will always be
No matter where I roam

Steel Mills, Basketball, The Lake
Are some of the things it's got
Serbians, Mexicans, Blacks and Poles
Thus the nickname, "The Melting Pot"

'Though I've been gone for many a year
The mem'ries will always stay
And I'm so glad I can always go home
No matter how far I stray
— Warren G. Landrum, Jr.

Anyhow, back to the memories...

I've been reading these posts for the past few days trying to come up with words I could add to these very touching stories. I agree with what everyone had to share! Particularly what Larry Payne said about our world is regressing instead of Progressing! I live in California and there is so much racial tension, not only amongst Blacks & Hispanics, but there has been a lot of same race crime against each other. It saddens me to see we have come to this point. Where did we go wrong? What happened along the way that changed the love and the diverse acceptance we once had? I constantly teach my son the importance of accepting everyone. I also teach him that he may not be accepted by all, and that's okay, but to always believe in himself. Don't allow anyone to make him believe that just because he's Black that he can't be successful or that he's not enough. It is an honor to witness this Presidential race that now includes an African-American ! Wow, who would ever thunk it!! We grew up being taught of slavery, we were also taught to get along with everyone. My parents were not bitter about how they grew up, therefore they were able to instill in us respect toward another, ESPECIALLY an adult. So many kids nowadays have NO respect for adults. I teach my son that it is not an option as to whether or not he will respect the teacher or authority figures......he will and that's that! Or he knows I'm old school parent and I will lay it on him if I ever hear or see him disrespect adults. What I'm trying to say people is that, how can we get back what we had? Most parents nowadays don't want you saying anything to their kids and if you do, the kids may fight you or shoot you! The racial tension in Los Angeles between Blacks & Hispanics is so strong that I hesitate sending my son to a multi-racial

environment where the population is majority Hispanic. Why? Not because I'm racist, but because these kids have not been taught any better and I fear risking my son's life because ignorance prevails! I know I'm rambling, and I wanted to put my 2 cents in some where, but I am grateful for the upbringing I had. My mother was mean, was a very strong disciplinarian.... at times I thought I hated her, but of course, once I grew up, I realized she instilled some very strong and useful skills in me. I respect my elders, I don't dislike because of race and I know that I am okay just the way I am... BLACK & BEAUTIFUL. The old saying goes.......Each one, Teach one....so if we reach out to the kids, maybe we stand a chance at making it better....not perfect.....but better! ((((hugs to all my ECW alumni)))))). Thanks for letting me share! Peace
Veda Johnson, July 3, 2008
1977 - 1979

Larry: That's right. We were friends, neighbors, classmates, and teammates, but most of all we knew each other very well. Many of us were in school together as long as 12 years (some of us from K through 12). Our families and relatives lived in the same town if not the same neighborhood. Sometimes right next door or across the street from each other.

Our friends were invited to our homes for dinner, sleepovers and even a few of my friends went with me to family reunions. When you don't get to know people, and have a true desire to learn of their culture; it develops into fear and ignorance and that's what turns ugly.

We were blessed to have grown up in EC. It was unique
Ceretha (Faye) Dukes-Howard, August 3, 2008
1962 - 1968

Boy, I love the fact that I grew up in a diverse city. My children attend School in Merrillville and even though it is only 17 miles from East Chicago, they haven't the slightest clue about diversity. These teachers are in it for a Paycheck. When I grew up, I really wasn't aware of racial differences. Times have changed. It is so unfortunate. I believe that before a teaching degree is awarded , that teacher needs to be able to pass assessments qualifying or helping them realize if they have any racial differences. It has to be taught to children at an early age. We can't go back, but we can move forward and embrace and respect each other as People... not as Black People or White People, just as ordinary people...

Ursula Peppers, August 8, 2008
1984—1986

One of the bright spots in my life was the diversity in East Chicago or Indiana Harbor. I do remember as a child I could not walk through Sunnyside or New Sunnyside until later. I remember my first babysitter was Polish (Helen Butewicz) and I spoke Polish as a child. Patricia Butewicz (Helen's daughter) taught me jump rope. I have lived all over the world and my respect of culture is based on my Indiana Harbor upbringing.

Most people found it strange that an African American female could speak Russian. I can thank my teacher Paul Demkovich (sp) for that.

Debra Darcel Gil, August 10, 2008
1966 - 1969

In some brief words, I wish I could go back because I truly loved our town, I loved all my friends, I loved the fact that my first friend when I was four was Lithuanian, the second Polish, the third African-American, the fourth Mexican, the fifth, Armenian, the sixth Puerto Rican, and then Serbian, Slovak..lol. The best thing? I didn't even realize what all these descriptions meant until I was in about the sixth grade, lol. It was really cool to learn everyone's customs and traditions. I mean where else in the world could you get a group of brothers named, Puente, Jacque, Smilgius, Arzumanian, Bieniak, Rodriguez, Barnett, Kurmis, Lopez, Humco, Broomes, Page, Santiago, etc....

It was great. I wish my kids could've experienced it.

Anthony Puente, December 2, 2008
1979 - 1983

I wish that I could of appreciated East Chicago back then like I do now. I didn't learn about different races until 6th grade and even then it wasn't a big deal. Everybody took care of everybody. That is the way it is supposed to be all the time.

Tyna L. Findley (Joshua), December 1, 2008
1982 - 1986

Well, hopefully, after reading some of the remembrances from my fellow Senators in this chapter, you can begin to get some kind of idea about what a truly miraculous place we all were raised in. As everyone said, we were all in it together, and most of us never experienced any kind of racial prejudice until we moved away from The Harbor.

With the recent election of Barack Obama as the 44th President and 1st African-American President of the United States on November 4th, 2008, and with the racial climate in America as it is today, if average Americans of all races could take a look at some of these stories and use them as examples to build upon, we would truly take a huge step as a nation to move toward the type of America that President Obama envisions—an America of One People. It's like my wife, who is from Jamaica said, when quoting her country's slogan—"Out of Many, One". If America could steal that slogan and embrace it, that would help us realize our true potential as a nation as well, because it definitely applies to us.

Chapter 5

Growing up in The Harbor—Prelude

"The Harbor" section of East Chicago, Indiana was no Mayberry. But it was no Chicago or LA or New York either—although you could probably plop The Harbor down in the midst of one of those large cities and Harborites could blend right in. But The Harbor I grew up in probably WAS more like Mayberry than Chicago, at least back in the 60's and 70's when I was growing up there. You might not see Opie or Goober Pyle or Andy or any of those characters, but there WERE some characters to be seen. I'm talking about Black and White and Latino characters. We had 'em all, and we had a good mix of sub-cultures within each of these groups. Of course, that whole era was a lot simpler and safer and we moved at a much slower pace than what's happening there in today's day and age. So I want to take you back to that time and that place and try to give you a sense of what the kids of that time were doing as they went about their day-to-day duties of just being a kid. The only disclaimer I will make is that, of course, I can only give this view from my own perspective, filtered by my own experiences and remembrances of what I went through and peppered by remembrances of the friends, classmates, relatives, associates, and bullies that I grew up with. If you asked someone else to tell you about THEIR time in The Harbor, obviously you'd get a totally different story. Especially, if that person happened to have grown up on the 'wrong' side of the law or was some type of juvenile delinquent. If you're looking for a story with a Fonzy-like perspective, this is probably the wrong book for you. But someone has to write the story of the "Good Kid". And although it might not be as exciting or bloody or dangerous as the story of a thug might be, I'm sure it's a story that a lot of you can relate to, because, after all, I believe the majority of kids who grew up in America during that time, probably went through some of the same basic types of pleasures; and when all is said and done, we were all (or most everyone I knew) just trying to make it into and out of our teens and into adulthood so that we could hurry up and be grown, and go out and make our mark in the world. So come along with me—while I indulge…

Growing up in The Harbor— Prelude

What Was Going On

1970—1974

Year	Top Song Grammies - Record of the Year, Artist - R & B Song of the Year, Artist	
1970	Aquarius/Let The Sun Shine In	The Fifth Dimension
	Color Him Father	The Winstons
1971	Bridge Over Troubled Water	Simon and Garfunkel
	Patches	Clarence Carter
1972	It's Too Late	Carole King
	Ain't No Sunshine	Bill Withers
1973	The First Time Ever	Roberta Flack
	Papa Was a Rolling Stone	The Temptations
1974	Killing Me Softly	Roberta Flack
	Superstition	Stevie Wonder

Year	Oscar-Winning Movie	Other Movies
1970	Patton	The Great White Hope
1971	The French Connection	Shaft
1972	The Godfather	Lady Sings The Blues / Super Fly
1973	The Sting	The Exorcist / The Mack
1974	The Godfather, Part II	Blazing Saddles / Uptown Saturday Night

Year	TV Drama Emmy	TV Comedy Emmy
1970	Marcus Welby, M. D.	My World and Welcome To It
1971	The Bold Ones	All in the Family
1972	Elizabeth R.—Masterpiece Theatre	All in the Family
1973	The Waltons	All in the Family
1974	Upstairs, Downstairs—Masterpiece Theatre	M*A*S*H

Chapter 6

Growing up in The Harbor

Warren Remembers

Comic Books

For me, from the time I was about seven or eight years old until about the time I got into high school and discovered partying and girls, it was all about two things basically:

> 1) Comic Books
> 2) Playing Basketball in the Streets and Alleys

I have to admit that by the time I got into high school, I had one of the biggest comic book collections in The Harbor. I believe that only Tony Ulloa and Jorge Cisneros had comparable amounts of comics at that time. I knew of all of the main comic book stores in The Harbor. There was Virgil's on 140th and Alder, Dino's on 140th and Main Street, Pete's & Bruno's on 139th and Main Street, and that one over on the 3800 block of Pulaski, (Maravillas) that used to sell used comics. There was also a used comic book store over on Broadway, a couple blocks before you got to Euclid.

Now I didn't get into those fluff-fluff comic books much—ones like Richie Rich, and Archie and Casper the Friendly Ghost and Little Lotta, that fat girl. But obviously, as you can tell since I know some of their names, I may have bought an issue or two or three of them along the way. But the REAL comics, the ones that separated the boys from the girls and Grown-up boys from Little boys were produced by two main comic book factories—DC Comics and Marvel Comics.

Some of the most famous DC Comics characters were Superman, Batman, The Flash, Wonder Woman, Green lantern, Green Arrow, and Aquaman, all of whom were members of The Justice League of America. Of course, Superman and Batman have gone on to have many television shows and movies made about them.

But the Marvel side of the comic-book world, aka 'The Marvel Universe' was the best, as far as I was concerned. Marvel Comics had characters who had real problems and emotions and just seemed more real. The art at Marvel was probably a cut above that at DC as well. Looking back on it, adding to my preference of Marvel Comics probably was the fact that most of the characters, with the exception of Captain America, (who first showed up in 1941 during World War II) debuted in the early 1960's—my formative comic-reading years, and so I was able to grow up with a lot of them from day One. Indeed, I had most of the first issues for most of the characters like: The Fantastic Four, Spider-Man, The Hulk, Daredevil, Iron Man, The X-Men, The Mighty Thor, The Silver Surfer, Captain America, The Avengers and Sgt. Fury and The Howling Commandos, amongst many others.

As I said, by the time I left high school, I had over a thousand issues of comics, easily. By the time I enlisted in the US Air Force, and went off to Germany, most of these had made it to my parents' garage at the back of our house for 'safekeeping'. So you can imagine my horror and dismay when I came back from Germany and returned home, only to find out that my mother had thrown all of my comics away! Each and every one of them! I was devastated and quite honestly, pissed off at my mother for a few years after that. But knowing that I could never rebuild a collection that came even close to matching the one she had destroyed, I effectively ended my career as a comic book collector, and reluctantly entered the adulthood phase of my life.

Basketball

Comic books were not the only thing that took up my time when I was growing up. If you lived in Indiana, and especially if you lived in East Chicago (or so I thought) basketball was KING ! From the time I got my first basketball from The Inland Steel Christmas Party at about the age of 3 or 4, until the day I tore my Achilles tendon playing basketball in the back yard of my best friend George, about 35 years later, I guarantee you, there was never too much time that would pass from the time of my last basketball game to the next one.

As little kids, we grew up in the parks and alleys all over The Harbor, playing basketball. For me, it didn't matter if I was by myself, or playing with others in a pickup game, it seems like I was ALWAYS on some basketball court. There was many a day when my mother would have to send someone to get me from Sunnyside Park, a couple blocks away, so I could come home and eat dinner. Or worse yet, she or someone would have to get me late at night, because I'd be playing until the lights went out, even if it was nothing but shooting lay-ups or jump shots by myself. Needless to say, if my mother had to come get me herself, that meant a big-time whipping when I got home. And depending on how mad she was, it might even start on the way home!

But for the most part, George and I were inseparable. As long as we had a ball or could get to the parks or alleys together, it was "game on". Most times, we'd wind up playing one-on-one until other people showed up. And then it usually went like this. If you got one more person that came out, you'd probably switch to a game of HORSE or Twenty-One until someone else joined, so that all three of you could play at the same time.

As any basketball junkie knows, HORSE is played by the first player shooting, and if he makes the shot, the next player has to make the same shot. If that 2nd player makes it, then the 3rd player has to make it. If the 3rd player makes it, it goes back to the 1st player and he has the lead again. Whenever someone misses, they get a letter, starting with H, and when you get all 5 letters, H-O-R-S-E, you are out. Last player left wins.

And twenty-one is played by making baskets until one person reaches twenty-one—counting one point for each made basket. You usually could not shoot lay-ups until you reached some pre-determined number of points, usually eleven, but sometimes fifteen, depending on the rules set at the beginning of that game. When you reached eleven, you then got to shoot as many free throws as you could until you missed. It was every man for himself for rebounds and shots.

So we'd play one-on-one, or HORSE or twenty-one until we had enough guys to at least play a two-on-two or three-on-three half-court game. Sometimes, when we were playing in the alleys, it was so tight, that's all you had room for—a half-court game. Or you might just have one basket nailed up to a telephone pole or to the back of somebody's garage. Or sometimes, we didn't even have baskets—we'd just use those big empty barrel garbage cans as the basket, retrieving the ball out after each made shot!! So you'd have to dribble through broken glass, or maybe dribble behind a parked car to let it set a pick for you, and knock down a jumper from thirty-feet out. If they would have had the three-point basket back when I was growing up, some of the scores would have probably been in the high hundreds, because we had some guys who could really shoot the long J's—guys like Moocho and Tommie Lee come to mind.

If we finally got enough guys to play full court, and happened to be in a park that had an open full court, it was GAME ON—for real! This is where we got serious and you'd see some moves or dunks on the playground that would put NBA stars in awe! I remember that Butney, one of the playground legends at Sunnyside Park, used to tell me, 'Lil Bro, you're dunking off the wrong foot', and then he would crack up laughing. But I didn't really care, because I must have been all of about 5'8 or 5'9" at the time, and I was happy to be dunking off of ANY foot!

As I got older, I got to stray farther and farther to play street ball. First it was Sunnyside Park, then Baby Park over on Butternut Street about 4 or 5 blocks away. Then I got to go over to Washington Park a little further away. They had some good competition and games over on Drummond and

Carey Street too, but I didn't go on those streets too much, because I was from 'cross-town' and we were not really welcome back there. That's where the so-called 'bad kids' and 'thugs' were. My best friend George moved to Carey Street when we were about ten or so, I guess, so I'd go over to his house to play or get him so we could hit the parks—but that was about the extent of my time on Carey Street.

As we got even older, we'd grab our bikes and ride across the Viaduct to a part of town called Nu-Addition. The kids in Nu-Addition all went to our arch rival High School, East Chicago Roosevelt, so there was not much love lost between them and us. Although we had some tough, physical games with them, most of the times, there were no fights—at least no more than at any other park. But on the courts was where you could earn your respect. Even if you did not wind up playing organized ball for our school (Washington High Senators) or theirs (Roosevelt High Rough Riders), you could still earn a measure of respect on the court if you had game. And you could usually tell how much game you had during selection of teams. There would be two captains—usually the best players on the court that day—and they would take turns picking guys until each team had 5 members. If you were one of the first couple of guys picked, that meant you had game. If you were the last, that usually meant you were a scrub—unless there was just a whole bunch of talented guys at the park that day. I must admit that, even though I was a little bitty runt of a dude for most of my years growing up, I was seldom picked last. Because I could 'jump out of the gym' and had a pretty good knack for getting to the boards for rebounds, and for making unorthodox shots, I got my respect.

But of all of the parks in The Harbor, and probably in all of E.C. at that time, Sunnyside Park was the one to go to if you wanted some really 'serious' competition, or wanted to just watch some hard-core street basketball being played. People from Nu-Addition and Calumet, and even other cities, like Gary and Hammond, knew this as well. I remember that in the summers during my high school years, it would not be uncommon to see some of the guys from ECR's team come over by the car-full to challenge our guys like Jr. Bridgeman and Turk and Floyd and Wayne Williams and Darnell and Ruben, and some of our best street-ball players like Moocho and Butney to some serious hoops. Some of these challengers, like Jim Bradley and my cousin Wayne Hackett, played on Roosevelt's undefeated 1970 State Championship team. Then there were guys from Gary, who would also come over to see how they matched up against the best. These would be guys like Jimmy Harvey and Isaiah Clark, who later would play on Gary West Side's 1972 team that lost in the state championship game.

I used to say that the talent in East Chicago during the time I grew up was amazing. I also would tell people when I left the city that I could go back home and pick any four drunks or winos off the street and compete with any good junior college program in America and with SOME Division 1 programs. I was only half-joking.

Chapter 7

Growing Up in The Harbor

ECW Senators Remember

Now I'd like to go from sharing my own remembrances of what it was like growing up in The Harbor to sharing some from my fellow East Chicago Washington Senators. This should give you an even better idea of what life was like back then. All of the remembrances in this chapter are recounted as originally told in the 'Growing up in The Harbor' forum on the ecwonline.ning (2008) website.

Note: Some spelling and punctuation errors were corrected in the following remembrances, but none of the content or meaning of what was being said was altered. In some cases, the errors were left in to get across the true emotions that the person was putting out!

Additionally, you will note that some of the attendance dates listed are for more than 4 years. No, these people were not 'slow learners'. The Washington High Campus used to host grades 7 through 12 up until about the year I graduated, in 1972. So some folks just included their Jr. High attendance years, as well.

To me living and growing up in the Harbor, was the place to be. Boy did I have fun in them 'good ole days', going to school taking short cuts thru alleys, thru back yards, and getting there and standing outside the school talking to the girls till the bell rang! I never cut classes. Living and interacting with all classes of people was not a problem to me. I worked at a lot of places where I got to meet a whole lot of people, made many friends. OH, do I miss the ole HARBOR, and of course my good ole friends. Does anybody know anything about any reunion of class 1971? I was not a popular girl, but I did have friends. Anyway, I'm happy that my brother connected me with this new page. I will be sure to pass it along. Hopefully I will meet up with somebody from my class.... God bless you all. One more thing. I have fond memories of growing up in the Harbor. That is my home and growing up there was great. It has made me who I am.

Carmen Cruz, April 6, 2008
1967 - 1971

It laid the foundation of the person I've become. Racism was something on TV, until I moved away. There were no color barriers, just people. My God, I didn't realize any difference living in the Harbor. What a shock, call me naïve; I never realized how much hate the world has. I BECAME THE MINORITY!!!

The world hasn't changed much. We still struggle with the same issues. I am so grateful for my roots and what I've learned. It's definitely made me a better person!!!!!!!!!!!!!!

It was a wonderful time growing up in the Harbor!!!!!!!!!!!

Jenny Rodriguez, April 7, 2008
1974 - 1978

All the memories come rushing back. If I remember right, there were 4 theaters in the Harbor - The Garden, The American, The Vic and The Indiana. Back then you had two features, a cartoon and Coming Attractions. They played continuously and you didn't have to leave after the movie ended. If you were late for a movie, you just waited around and caught what you missed when they replayed it. Sometimes, I'd stay there all afternoon. I was telling my granddaughter one day about the old pop machines in the theater where you put your quarter in and the cup dropped down, then the syrup, the carbonated water and finally the ice. But, sometimes it didn't come out like that. Sometimes the cup came out last. I had her in stitches talking about that old pop machine. Green River was my favorite.

Larry Payne, August 24, 2008
1963—1967

There was the Little Wheel on Columbus Drive across the street from WHS. Sometimes they would add a bit-o-spit to the burgers for flavor. There was also Galic's on Columbus Drive also across the street from WHS. What a great candy store that was (after he closed his store for good, Tita opened her store). Around the 4th of July, Galic would sell firecrackers on the side if you could show an I.D. proving you were older than six years old.

Across the street from Washington Park was an empty field that we used to call the "prairie". It is now a parking lot for St Catherine's Hospital. We used to play baseball there in the 60's. I remember pitching to Ricky Masterson and getting hit straight in the mouth with a line drive (my head still hurts).

Talking about right across the street from Washington Park. There was also that house on 142nd St and Hemlock with the life size polar bear in the window. He would light it up at night and always leave the windows open so you could see it if you were passing by.

I remember there was a guy that used to have a hotdog cart right outside the drug store on "Busy Corner". It was always a good late night option

Anthony Lang, August 27, 2008
1972—1975

I remember swimming in the man made lake on Columbus Drive & Cline Avenue. Once, a couple of friends and I "found" a raft someone had made from about six utility poles. It was very sturdy but we found out too late that our sticks and brooms were useless for oars on something that big. After about 3 hours, we finally drifted to the other side. Got home real late & took a GOOD whoopin'. Don't know what excuse I used, but had I told the truth I might still be getting beat. Good thing my mom doesn't use computers. lol.

Winston Johnson, August 28, 2008
1973—1977

The other dress shop was Rothchilds. How about the items from DanDee Discount and the Silvercup Bread Factory on Main near Columbus Drive. I believe that was the name. Don't forget Gould's on Main Street, where we purchased the red or maroon gym suits. We looked great in suits the school parking lot during gym class playing kick ball. Remember the yearly gym events at Riley school in the elementary. Who was a patrol monitor along Columbus Drive between Euclid and Parrish again during

Washington Elementary Days? Remember, "Don't run" and "Wait for the crossing guard". Too Many Years Ago!
Elozia Ann Jernigan-Neeley, August 29, 2008
1964 - 1969

OH MY GOD!

I just had to write something on this page. I remember walking to Harbor Foods 'cause my mom and dad made the groceries there. When I met my now husband, we would go to the Hiawatha restaurant on Michigan Avenue to eat their famous Hamburger Deluxe! When we wanted to eat Mexican food, it was off to The Patio. I was raised on Deodar Street right across the street from OLG Church even though I didn't attend much. On Main Street was the great Shrimp House where me and my boyfriend walked over to buy their famous fries with hot sauce. Those were great times and ones I'll never forget!
Azalia 'Sally' Castro, August 30, 2008
Class of '78
1974—1978

I tease my mom, because back in the day, Bridgette Gibson, Belinda Green, Deneen Walton, myself, Jean, Rhonda, Joann Lofton and others - used to play on the train tracks. We would wait for a train to come, and right before it got near us, we would go & run and put a penny on the tracks. Was that dangerous or what??? But that was playing for us. I always tease my mom and say "Why you let us play on the tracks?" - and we weren't even "Ghetto" back then, just good ole fun. And I remember playing "kick soccer" till late at night, "kick the can", and just hanging out on our porches on Guthrie Street. And remember when the K House used to have those talent shows? I was always in the cooking classes there. Boy, those were the days!

Gwendolyn (Aikens) Upshaw, September 1, 2008
1981 - 1985

Yeah, I grew up in Da Harbor. And I worked at the Grill Restaurant, the unemployment office, and, oh let me not forget the theatre, the Garden Theatre. That old man used to pay us girls 50 cents an hour!!! But at least we used to get in after 9 to watch what ever they were showing (in Spanish of course) for FREE!! I loved going into Newberry's. THEY HAD EVERYTHING A KID COULD WANT! Especially the dolls. Nothing moved, then when the dolls came out moving their hands and legs, there were the tiniest rubber bands holding them from one side to the other. Boy, they were hard to put back when they came off!!! lol. Those were the days! Do you all remember the candy store on Fir Street off Broadway, going towards 136th Street, near the alley? Ms. Muffs Candy store? Now let me tell you, for 50 cents you got a BAG FULL OF CANDY!! And the cheese popcorn bags were only 5 cents! I walked home happy with all that candy....

Carmen Cruz, September 3, 2008
1967 - 1971

Do you all remember summer gym at "The Dub"? Man you talkin' about fun! What about the summer lunch program, trying to get a summer job, the K-House, Baby Park (Callahan Park) across from the Lincoln building, catching a ride on the trains behind the Guthrie buildings, playing kick the can, hide the belt, hide and go get it, IT, freeze tag, pickles, the dozens (Yo mama so fat.....) LOL, water balloon fights, swimming at Washington Park, Spann picnics, playing ball for the recreation centers (Clemente, Penn, Tod, 151rst) during the summer, swimming at Clemente pool (rally off the diving board), house parties, catching the bus to go to Screamin' Wheels, Baldy leavin' your butt because you went to the McDonalds and the line was long as hell and you saying "I can make it"? LOL. Alright, let me stop. I'm gettin' all choked up. The GOOD OLD DAYS!! I miss them.

Charles Sanders, September 6, 2008
1982—1986

I remember working at Zel's my freshman year. Coach Flores spoke to Mr. Demkovich and got me a job at Sears { Southlake Mall}. I was making more money but my excuse for not making weight was gone. I kept that job all through school and never missed weight again. This is one of the many ways I'm indebted to some of the staff members at ECW. Teachers as part of our community and caring about the total person, not just the student are some of the reasons the Harbor was a special place.

Winston Johnson, September 6, 2008
1973 - 1977

What wonderful memories they were when I was a little one... My dad taking my sisters and I for a walk to Dino's for Sundaes and Chili Dogs from John's Eat Shop. There was a field behind my house (Sunnyside) before they built that trucking company. I loved climbing those trees, and hiding in the tall grass with my cousins. Sunnyside Park had the tall brown monkey bars, Jack and Jill slide, and that huge slide that was still scary to the bravest kid. And the winter ice skating and sledding...

Lenora Franco, September 7, 2008
1978—1982

Ok. I remember The Harbor very well. I lived on the corner of 4001 Pulaski. I lived across the street first at 4002 Pulaski. We lived on top of Manuel's, a great corner store and I remember Dino's very well. And who can forget Main Shrimp House. I remember Eddie and Rick Garcia working there - and Michael Quiroz. I used to hang out with Michael all the time and as far as Crazy Louie, his name was Luis Deleon, he was related to a dear friend of mine named Lupe. Now I wonder what ever happened to them. The Harbor was a nice place to live at one time. Now I hear so much bad things. And that is real sad ... I wish we can do something about that and clean The Harbor and East Chicago up. It's too much gangs now and nobody cares. Maybe we can put a big community group together and see if we can do something. IM IN... I remember Rothschild's on Main Street. I would go with my mom all the time ☺. But I also remember a lot that happened there and it brings bad memories in my life. But all considered, I grew up ok and happy now, so The Harbor will always be a memory in my life and I carry it everywhere I go...

Diane Casas, September 9, 2008
1980—1984

When I think back on those days, I can say with a smile they were some of the most wonderful times I had in my life. East Chicago had some of the best food places to eat at. My special places were Shrimp Harbor, John's Eat Shop - for their chili dogs, Zel's - Roast Beef, & chili dogs, Taco Delight - sopes, soft tacos, hard tacos, and the donuts from the bakery on Main Street. I loved skipping down the streets, playing softball at the parks with my friends, and marching in the parades with Junior Police as a drill team member and Washington High School Band asa Majorette. I think *singing and dancing at the old folks homes during the holidays was one of my favorites. To see the smiles on their faces when we would perform for them was a blessing to me that I will always cherish. But my all time favorite was spending Saturday mornings with my Grandmother. She started the morning cooking my favorite breakfast, which was bacon, eggs, grits and toast with strawberry jam, and she sang old church songs while she cooked. Then she would comb my hair. It was always shorter than my sisters' hair. They had braids down their back and my hair could hardly hold the rubber band because it was so curly and shorter, but my Grandmother would always tell me that I had a special kind of hair, and one day it would grow to be just as long as my sister, so I would smile and walk around with that crazy hairdo that she gave me for years. (smile)*

Annette (Sessions) Ortega, September 13, 2008
1974 - 1977

There are 4 spots I used to hang out at with my friend Millicent.

1. We would go to see Major Seay at Max Blumfield Jewelers.

2. Cook's Record Shop

3. Chicken Unlimited. We used to stay in there until they would tell us we had to leave.

4. We would go to the A&P store with Millie's neighbor to help her with her groceries and instead of candy we would convince her to buy us a bottle of TJ Swann wine.

(((((((((((MEMORIES!!!!!!!))))))))))))))

Vilma Gonzalez, September 17, 2008
1977—1981

Do you remember the best ice cream truck in the world with the banging ice cream? But dude had an attitude...he would rush you, but we kept coming back... Remember the vegetable man in the pickup truck?? The milkman left the milk and juice outside the door and collected the bottles?? Calumet Newspaper on Broadway? It was free but I use to sale it ... and the Latin Times (lol)... Had to get my ice cream hustle on!!! Hiawatha Restaurant, hot dog stand in front of Busy Corner (Nobles) and taco stand. Sandwiches from Harry's store with potato chips and pop. Remember French Fries and gravy... hot sandwiches... John Eat's Chili Dogs? In '83, you could get 2 chili dogs, fries and coke for $2.00... Quick route to Katherine House Boys Club through Mademoiselles when it was cold... I could go on and on.....WHAT HAPPENED TO OUR CITY... THAT'S SAD!!!
      Anibal "Nebo" Gonzalez, September 26, 2008
                1981—1985

Hey, everyone... You must have forgotten that we had two dime-stores on Main Street in The Harbor and another one in East Chicago on Chicago Avenue. When I was growing up, (Block and Pennsy) the Indiana Show would let you in for free on your birthday. They would have wonderful scary movies on Halloween which really scared us kids. I used to work at all of the movie theaters except the Indiana, and let my friends in for free... We used to sneak in the French Fries from the deli next to the American theater. Bobbie's was another corner store. I believe it was on Block Avenue, not too far from Eugene Field School. Yes, Inland Steel would have their Christmas parties for the families at WHS and I remember Riverview in Chicago, which the Inland Steel families always looked forward to visiting... Growing up in The Harbor, especially on Block and Pennsy, left me wonderful memories... then again, when we are young, we do not think the way we do now that we are older...yet we had fun and created wonderful memories with the different diversity of people from different countries. Memories and friends are precious. Yes, our children and grandchildren still do not believe we lived the way we did. Today I can't live without my air-conditioner and computer... how about you? To think we lived without all these conveniences then... ahhhhh what a life!!

Conception (Flores) Bueno, October 8, 2008
1962 - 1965

For those of us who lived near the 39th block of Carey Street, we had Byrd's candy store. It was like a throw back to the 1950's. On the 38th block of Carey, we had another candy story that I started to go to after Byrd sold his store to someone who was dealing drugs out of it and it got raided. Sweet memories of youth!

Remember when Zel's was at the original location in the building next door and they had a walk up window? They used to put the ketsup on the fries for you. Back in the day, East Chicago did not have a McDonald's, so the Dairy Queen was king. Remember the orange glow of the night sky from the Zinc Oxide that should not have been released by the steel mills? Remember how small your elementary school was when you went back to it? ECW may be gone, but it is not forgotten. It will never shrink in our reality of time and space since we cannot visit the bricks and mortar. It will grow in legend as we breathe life into it again and again with our shared experiences. Life is good, family is great and Washington Senators are legends.

Jacqueline Smith, October 13, 2008
1979 - 1983

Who remembers the Bus system? We would catch the bus at Walgreen's on Main and Broadway and ride to downtown Gary or Hammond. And then in Hammond we would go to the Show there or go to GOLDBLATT'S. I remember in Walgreen's, they used to have the food counter, and most all the drugstores had a soda fountain.

And Shrimp Harbor - to get a bag of fries with the sauce and a pop for about 50 cent... What about the Pool Hall on Broadway where the Legendary "Scoffy Duck" would sit blood drunk and motionless?

The shoe shop next to Art's Store for Men that was next to the Garden where we would get that GREEN RIVER. Do they make that pop anymore?

Greg "Chico" Davis, October 13, 2008
1969—1973

I remember catching the bus many weekends with my grandmother. Goldblatt's was my favorite. I'd help the elevator operator until she got tired of me hanging around, then I'd go to their HUGE toy dept and play with everything. Nobody seemed to care as long as we didn't get too loud. Of course, we always had lunch at the counter and managed to talk our way into various snacks before heading home. For a moment, I thought I was a kid again. What a carefree time!

Winston Johnson, October 15, 2008
1973—1977

Part of that shopping bus trip to Hammond was going to get White Castle hamburgers. Either there, or over in Whiting on your way back from Chicago. I'm Class of 61'. When we were going to school, hamburgers were 12c. To this day, when I come to EC, I have a list of food I have to have before I come home. White Castle hamburgers (they don't sale them on the west coast), taco's from a good Mexican restaurant, Zel's and shrimp .

I have enjoyed the walk down memory lane.

                              Helen Smith, November 9, 2008
                                            1956 - 1961

I know what you mean. I've GOT to have my White Castles when I go back to The Harbor. In addition to the 2 you're talking about over in Whiting and in Hammond, did you know that EC has it's own White Castle now? It's on Guthrie down at the end right before you make that right turn on that curve to go onto Cline Avenue. I used to live on Fern Street and boy, do I wish they had that one there when I was growing up! That's only a couple blocks away.

Also used to go over to Calumet to get my shrimp at Homer's Shrimp House. I know it might be talking treason, but I think Homer's was even better than the Broadway Shrimp house down there on Main off Broadway.

                        Warren Landrum, November 15, 2008
                                      1968 - 1972

Hey Guys,

Do any of you all remember Taco Joe's ? Way back in the back of my memory, I seem to remember this rumor about Taco Joe's and their CAT-MEAT tacos ! I think it was over in the Block and Pennsy area and I seem to remember that these were the best tacos in town. This must have been in the early 60's cause I was probably about 8 or 9.

I wanted to put this out there to you guys, so I'll know for sure about this before I die, and know that I did not just hallucinate that whole thing !!

Warren Landrum, October 25, 2008
1968—1972

DONT WORRY, I HEARD ABOUT THAT TOO AND IT WAS ON THE AREA YOU MENTIONED. I WONDER IF MY DAD BROUGHT US SOME HOME TO EAT. YOU KNOW THOSE INLAND STEELERS, GETTING HOME LATE BUT MAKING IT UP TO OUR MOMS BY BRINGING HOME SOMETHING TO EAT.

Gerardo Gaitan, October 25, 2008
1972 - 1976

Yeah Warren, I remember Taco Joe's. I Went to Field Elementary and 7th through 8th grade at E.C.W. with his son Joe Alvaredo, Jr. Joe Jr. left us and graduated from Bishop Noll High

William "Joey" France, November 2, 2008
1964 - 1970

Do you guys remember the Nifty Burger on Broadway where the Broadway Shrimp is located? They were imitating White Castle's Hamburgers. How about the Hot Tamale Man riding through town on that bike with the box on the front screaming Tamales, Hot Tamales?!. I know this one will stump a lot of you. How about Maravilla's Store on Pulaski Street, where you could get your groceries on account. We had credit and didn't know what credit was back then. You get groceries today and pay him next week. He would write the amount in one of those bookkeeping books and erase it when you come to pay. How about the Mexican Bakery, on Alder I believe it was?

They had what we called Turtle rolls and those pink, yellow and white cookies that were so soft and good. Man I finally found some at a Mexican bakery in Nashville. Couldn't compare...

Janice Johnson, October 15, 2008
1966 - 1971

Something about Mr. Frank Maravilla. God Bless this man. He was good to many people in The Harbor who couldn't quite make ends meet close to payday. He would give families credit on a little nickle notebook that was basically "your word" that you would pay. To the best of my knowledge, he still has his shop on Main Street.

Carlos Longoria, October 27, 2008
1965—1968

No. Just recently they sold out and just the other day I drove pass and all the buildings there are torn down now. From Albert's Jewelry to where Cook's Records was at. Maravilla was the last standing there till just recently. But that is sad to see all that torn down and supposedly they are to be making room for the new and improved "<u>Main St.</u>" . That is all fine and dandy, but bring back business. Do not push them to go to other cities, towns or what have you. Keep them here in The Harbor. Just like I found the other day that <u>Fuentes, a Mexican store</u> that has good fresh meat there is moving and is being sold out by the city and moving to Hammond. That made me sad and mad - sad because they are leaving and I like to go there to buy things - and mad because why didn't the city offer them another place? I am sure there is a lot of room in the city for them to build new and bigger and stronger but that seems to be the motto now in East Chicago. That the

Mayor is running people out of business, it just saddens me.... That is my thoughts!!!!!
Lisa Minjarez, October 30, 2008
1983 - 1986

After reading all the replies I felt like I was back in The Harbor again. I think everyone went to Dino's for ice cream at one time or another... went to the show on Saturdays... I remember the penny candy store next to Mike's... Was that a malt shop or what? Olympia restaurant and Los Burritos after the games... shopping on Main Street, buying shoes or looking for outfits at Mademoiselle's or Rothchilds... I remember the Zoo at Washington park.... When I think about it... The Harbor had it going on... Funny how things have changed... EC finally got a McDonalds and a Burger King....lol. I also remember going bowling, and shopping at Dandee Discount center... My mom used to take me to the Grill Restaurant on Sundays after church.... Great memories... Guess we will have lots to talk about at a reunion for the class of '69...
Dorothy Marijanovich Rybicki, November 12, 2008
1965—1969

I agree to what everyone else has said about feeling like we grew up without racial boundaries and just having fun. It was a shock to me at first as a student at Purdue Lafayette and sometimes at work that I am different. But in my heart and because I believe that we are all children of the same GOD that loves us all and teaches us to love each other, I know better. EC, the good times: open lunch when we used to run to Zel's or the Shrimp house for fries w/ mild sauce on it (they were soaked with it!), hanging out at the Lake front, making a bonfire at the Pits, or summer volleyball in that hot gym.

I am proud to say that I still live in EC. I chose to live and stay here. I still enjoy walks, the parks, going to church, playing volleyball, the festivals, the parades, and am looking forward to my nephew starting t-ball this summer. I've lived in other places and with my job, I travel often and am bless that I've been able to take a few vacations, and as wonderful as it is to go away once in awhile, it's always nice to come home. Just like a family, it's not perfect; we have our faults; and we have things that have happened that we're not proud of, but we have to accept, love, and help each other to move on and to try to make things better. Thanks, Kenny, for this website that allows us to hold on to good memories and, if only for a little bit, allows us to come back home!

Maria E. Porras, April 9, 2008
1982 - 1985

Chapter 8

Youngstown Sheet & Tube

Steel Dust in your too-black lungs
Shift work week to week
Union versus Company
More benefits you seek

Twenty-Three years of sweat and smoke
Working on that tin mill line
And there's only fifteen more to go
Before you've served your time

Yeah, fifteen long, long years to go
For that Gold Watch in your hand
And you'll hear them as you pass the gate
Say, 'Send the next man in!'

Youngstown Sheet & Tube

Younstown Sheet & Tube—Indiana Harbor Works

What Was Going On

1975—1979

Year	Top Song Grammies - Record of the Year, Artist - R & B Song of the Year, Artist	
1975	I Honestly Love You	Olivia Newton-John
	Living for the City	Stevie Wonder
1976	Love Will Keep us Together	The Captain and Tennille
	Where is The Love	Donny Hathaway/ Roberta Flack
1977	This Masquerade	George Benson
	Lowdown	Boz Scaggs
1978	Hotel California	The Eagles
	You Make Me Feel Like Dancin'	Leo Sayer
1979	Just The Way You Are	Billy Joel
	Last Dance	Donna Summer

Year	Oscar-Winning Movie	Other Movies
1975	One Flew Over the Cuckoo's Nest	Dog Day Afternoon
1976	Rocky	Taxi Driver
1977	Annie Hall	Star Wars
1978	The Deer Hunter	The Wiz
1979	Kramer vs. Kramer	Apocalypse Now

Year	TV Drama Emmy	TV Comedy Emmy
1975	Upstairs, Downstairs—Masterpiece Theatre	The Mary Tyler Moore Show
1976	Police Story	The Mary Tyler Moore Show
1977	Upstairs, Downstairs—Masterpiece Theatre	The Mary Tyler Moore Show
1978	The Rockford Files	All in the Family
1979	Lou Grant	Taxi

Chapter 9

The Mills

The poem that I wrote in the last chapter was written to my Dad and was included in my first book, "The Heart & Soul of a Black Man". It talked a little about what the essence of working in the steel mills is all about. You really can't talk about East Chicago or The Harbor without talking about The Mills. I know, personally, I had my Dad and both his brothers working in the mills, and on my mother's side of the family, there were numerous aunts and uncles and cousins working in them. And later on, before my senior year in High School, I even spent the summer in one of them, as did my baby sister, when she got old enough to do so. I would estimate that the great majority of my friends and schoolmates also had relatives working in the mills and a lot of them are still working in them today, some 35 years later, if they were fortunate enough not to get laid off. So, it was pretty much a way of life when we were growing up. The mills WERE The Harbor.

When you talked about the mills in East Chicago, you were primarily talking about the Big Two, which pretty much took up the whole shoreline of Lake Michigan between Whiting and Gary. Those were Inland Steel and Youngstown Sheet & Tube Company, and they took up most of the 2.3 square miles of water/harbor that was part of East Chicago's 15.6 square mile overall area.

Youngstown Sheet & Tube Company was actually created in 1900 in Youngstown, Ohio. Their factory that was located in The Harbor was actually formally called Youngstown Sheet and Tube—Indiana Harbor Works. It was created in 1923 when Youngstown out of Ohio purchased the facilities of The Steel and Tube Company of America in East Chicago. The acquisition of this 1200-acre plant made it the 5th largest steelmaker in America at that time. At its peak, Youngstown—Indiana Harbor Works, employed about 12,000 employees. So, as you can see, Youngstown was a major employer in a town that had a population ranging anywhere from about 25,000—30,000 over the last few decades.

Inland Steel was founded in 1893 through the purchase of a steel mill in Chicago Heights, Illinois—The Chicago Steel Works—by financier Joseph Block and his son Philip. In 1897, it built a large new open-hearth steel mill on the Indiana Harbor and Ship Canal on a large landfill extending out into Lake Michigan. and Inland Steel suddenly became a big business, growing from 250 workers in 1897 to 2600 in 1910. Employment at that mill would peak at 25,000 in 1969.

Between Youngstown and Inland Steel in The Harbor, and two mills over in Gary—U. S. Steel and Bethlehem Steel, those four accounted for about 30% of the steel production in the United States by the 1970's. They also had a most profound effect on the environment—giving our sky that constant 'orange haze' around it, which I guess was a result of the burning of all that ore and the oxides in the blast furnaces and what-not. I never even noticed this, growing up in it, not until I first went away to Purdue University in West

Lafayette, Indiana in the summer of '72 to start my college career. Boy, was I surprised when I returned home and noticed that you could just see this 'orange aura' hanging over The Harbor and Gary as you were on your way north up Interstate 65 and approached 'Da Region. There was also a pungent aroma that was unique to The Harbor that you never noticed when you were there, but could always smell when re-entering the town. If you were coming back into town from Chicago through Whiting, you'd always catch the smell of the oil refineries first coming up Highway 12, before you hit the back end of The Harbor over by where Youngstown met the refineries. Coming from the other direction, from Gary or Cline Avenue, you could smell it as soon as you got within a few miles of the mills. It would be interesting to see what the rate of lung cancer was in 'Da Region' or any other steel-producing parts of the country, for that matter, compared to other non-industrial parts of the U.S.. I don't have those numbers, but I'm sure it was much higher.

Inland Steel Christmas Parties

One of the highlights, if not THE highlight for kids, was Christmas-time, and that meant the Inland Steel Christmas party that was held at the East Chicago Washington gym every year, for Inland Steel employees and their families. They had performers, acrobats, magic and such—a lot of the same acts you'd see on The Bozo show on WGN, Channel 9! And they had lots and lots of presents. My Dad used to work at Youngstown, but he still would get lots of gift tickets from Inland every year (I think it's because he had some type of job with The Union). We'd actually get more gifts from Inland than we would get from Youngstown. I know I never had a shortage of basketballs around the house after an Inland Christmas Party!!

Here's what some of my fellow Senators remember about that:

LOVED the Christmas parties…except for the stockings. I vowed NEVER to get those for my children and thus I made stockings for all of us which we hang EVERY year. Our dog and cat even have their own stockings. I must admit, they HAVE received the red "gauze" ones in the past. My dad worked at Youngstown but we always seemed to get Inland tickets too. That was life in the Harbor! It was GREAT getting presents and I especially liked the trapeze ladies…they were awesome to a young wide-eyed girl! Thanks for taking me back to those wonderful days!
(Frankie) Francisca Flores Duenas, August 1, 2008
1977—1981

This was the greatest time when being able to see our very own "Circus" , clowns, flying trapezers and of course Santa Claus!!!! I miss those days…… Thanks for the memories. ECW !!!!
Elizabeth Santos Quinones, August 2, 2008
1979—1983

I loved the Inland Christmas Parties. It was such a treat to see the performers we saw on the Bozo Show. I clearly remember that children were not allowed in without their parents, so my sister, cousins and I would choose any family and stick close enough to make it look as if we belonged with them..:) I also remember wondering why there were four Santas - one on each corner entrance to the big gym. I always wondered which one was the real Santa:)

AH… childhood innocence.
> Damaris Torres, August 5, 2008
> 1974—1978

I remember the Inland Steel Christmas party the year after the strikes in the 1960's. The gift I received was the only gift that Christmas. I remember the food banquet!!! Does anyone remember the Boys Club near Guthrie and Michigan Avenue??? Those steel mill jobs really gave us the chance to become middle class and live the American dream.
> Debra Darcel Gil, August 11, 2008
> 1966—1969

Loved the show and gifts, but I could never figure out how there could be four different Santas—one in every corner of the balcony. And who were those kids that got to sit downstairs in the gym with Mr. Passmore. VIP's of the steel world? If so, why was I always left out? :)
> Jeanette Johnson Jackson, September 28, 2008
> 1961—1968 (7th—12th grade)

I loved going to the Inland Steel Christmas parties even though I was scared of heights and was scared out of my mind to climb the bleachers…lol. I remember my brothers getting basketballs and geez, I can't remember what I used to get. That was a highlight for us during the Christmas season. I also remember my dad taking us to Inland Steel to see the Christmas decorations and huge Christmas tree they had. They had music playing in the background. I just loved going there!
> Belinda Rangel, November 27, 2008
> 1978—1982

I could see I'm not the only one who likes to stroll down Memory Lane! I used to look forward to the Inland Steel Christmas party every year! How Blessed we were and we didn't even know it! What happened to companies taking care of the employees and their families ???

Richard Amescua, August 29, 2008
1984 - 1986

Chapter 10

Washington Park and Block Stadium

Washington Park

For a city as small as East Chicago, and a part of town as small as The Harbor, I have got to say that we had what MUST have been one of the most complete parks in the country. I was fortunate enough to spend some time in Central Park in New York last year, and I must say, that, as far as things to do, our Washington Park had just about as big a variety as Central Park! Add that to the fact that it was a lush, wooded cool place to spend some time with its winding trails. No wonder Washington Park seemed to be the happening place and the center of much of the outdoor entertainment that was going on in The Harbor back when I was a kid!

Washington Park was bounded by 142nd Street on the North, Grand Boulevard on the East, 144th Street on the South and Parrish Avenue on the West. Let's see—it had The Swimming Pool, The Concession Stand, The Tennis Courts, The Basketball Courts, The Greenhouses, lots and lots of picnic tables, a couple Softball Fields, and as I said, lots and lots of trees. I remember that if you were in certain parts of the park, and looked up, you couldn't even see the sky, because the trees and foliage were so dense.

But on top of this, the main thing that the park had that I remember as a little kid was The Zoo! It was only a small zoo, maybe one building, with two sides, with cages on each side, I believe, that sat off in the corner of the park. But it was a zoo, nonetheless, and it had BEARS! You can imagine how exciting that must have been for a little city kid to see a real live bear! I think they were black bears and there might have been 2 or 3 of them. But, however many of them there were, the point is we could go see them, less than 2 miles from our house, whenever we went to the park!

The zoo also had monkeys, snakes, and birds. That's all I can remember in detail. From what I understand, a tornado came through town one year and destroyed the zoo and they never opened it back up after that.

Anyhow, here's the question I asked and what some of my fellow Senators had to say about the zoo and the greenhouse when I asked them if they remembered them...

> *I have vague memories of the zoo that used to be over in that one corner of Washington Park - over on Parish Street, I believe. The only animals I remember seeing in it were a black bear, some monkeys, and some birds.*
>
> *I remember it was there - and then one day, the buildings were still there—but no animals. Anybody want to share memories about what kind of animals they saw there, or maybe what happened to it to make them close it??? Also, I seem to remember us going on a field trip from Franklin School, walking across the prairie (now Prairie Park) to*

the park and going inside a BIG greenhouse. Anybody remember that?

Warren Landrum, November 18
1968 - 1972

I believe at one time there was a lion and a tiger in the zoo. I think the animals were removed because there were problems with the upkeep. That's the story I heard.

Actually I think there were 2 greenhouses. We used to always go through them around the warm weather holidays, because they were always having plant and flower shows there. But, you could go there anytime and walk through them. There were always some exotic plants there.

Larry Payne, November 18, 2008
1963—1967

I grew up on Grand Blvd. a block from Washington Park. Some of my fondest memories are of my time spent there. I remember the bear and ducks and the two greenhouses. I also remember the cannon that was there near the bandstand. Oh, my, the bandstand... I remember having a tap-dancing recital there!

What I remember most is playing tennis at the park almost everyday in the summer. And listening to the songs on the jukebox and eating hotdogs and frozen treats from the concession stand. Man, those were the days. When I hear songs on the radio that I remember were on that jukebox, it takes me right back there, and I smile every time.

Lisa Lang, November 25, 2008
1973—1977

I remember the field trips across the prairie also. I also remember swimming at the pool at Washington Park and also at the lakefront. There used to be a concession stand at both and I had worked at both at one time. Music was always playing at both parks if I remember right. We even had a lifeguard at the lakefront...now you can't swim there. LOL. And Back Lake was the place for all the young lovers...hummm humm..

Darcel (Beaupain) Resto, November 23, 2008
1965 - 1970

Dear Warren,

I moved to Parrish Avenue directly across from the park when I was three years old in 1952. I, too, have vague memories of the zoo. It was shortly after I moved there that the zoo animals were removed. I remember bears and ducks and I sort of think that there may have been raccoons, but I'm not sure. I THINK there were lions there when I first saw the zoo; but they were inside and I didn't really see them. I read a story recently in the Anvil newsletter about the zoo. Evidently, one lady who moved to Parrish Avenue. was unaware that there were lions in the zoo. Maybe she was unaware that there even was a zoo in the park. Anyway, on her first night in her new home she was trying to fall asleep and heard them roaring! Can you imagine HER fright? That's about all I know about the zoo. It was pretty smelly and I recall feeling very sad for the bears, who seemed sad and despondent.

Sherry Shapiro Kessel, November 19, 2008
1962 - 1967

I, too, remember the zoo, the greenhouses, the cannon, and the bandstand. It was at one of those free talent shows that

I first saw the group known as The Jackson Five. It was waaaaay before their days of fame; I think Michael was four at the time and we were wondering if they could ever become as successful as The Sylvers (the other big afro family group of that era). We walked across the prairie from Franklin Elem., throwing "sticker bugs" on each other and pulling cat tails along the path. I moved the next year and went to Washington Elem. I also remember the swimming pool having girl's day and boy's day. Finally they went co-ed and I could tag along with my older brothers. Does anyone remember that mean old life-guard??? I think her name was Mrs. Zajack or something like that. She scared the living daylights out of me. Those WERE the days!

Jeanette Johnson Jackson, December 6, 2008
1961—1968 (7th—12th grade)

Yes, there was a bear. In fact there was a small zoo near the center of the park 'til about '66 or whenever the tornadoes came through. I remember some friends and I "survey-ing" the damage the next day or so. I'll never forget how big the trees were lying down.

Winston Johnson, September 11, 2008
1973 - 1977

Wow. So now we know what happened to the zoo. I did not know that EC even HAD tornados—although I do remember we had to go through those tornado drills in school, as a young kid, now that I think of it. The mem'ries just keep comin'…

But anyway… as I said, Washington Park had a lot going on in it. There were always big picnics in the parks around

holidays, and people would be picnicking out there just about any time during the summer months. There was this big-shot County Commissioner, Atterson Spann, who used to sponsor a big Fourth Of July (I think) picnic out at the park every year. There would be people from all over EC—from Nu-Addition and Calumet, as well as from The Harbor. I don't remember any violence with all these different folks mixing—just fun and good times.

It was at Washington Park that I saw The Jackson Five for the first time. They were from neighboring Gary, Indiana, and they came over to Washington Park from time to time. I remember when I saw them, they were actually set up and playing their gig on the tennis court. I'll never forget, I was hanging from one of the fences around the court to get a good view. I don' think they had blown up and become famous yet, because Michael couldn't have been over 4 or 5 years old at that time, it seems.

I also saw The Staples Singers at Washington Park. They were from Chicago, but they were really down to earth folks, especially Mavis, it seems. I remember later in life, she and Gospel Great Albertina Walker, would always stop by Ray's Golden Bird, where my mother worked, when they were in town. I guess they liked Ray and Tiny's greasy chicken ☺ !

I hadn't learned to swim yet back then, so the pool held no fascination for me. But I remember it was always pretty crowded.

One part of the park that DID hold an interest for me was the basketball courts, of course. They were right in front of the concession stand, outdoors on concrete, like most of the courts around town at the city parks. So that was another place for us to display our skills and have our wars whenever we happened to be at the park.

The other major part of the park was the softball fields. There were 2 softball fields on the end of the park right across the street from the Little League fields and Block Stadium. It was kind of funny the way they were laid out. If you picture a clock, home plate on one of the fields was at about at the 12 on the clock, whereas home plate for the other field was at 6 on the clock. There were no fences or anything separating the fields. So, if 2 games were going on at the same time, and someone from one field hit a long fly ball, it might wind up going past that field's outfield and into the infield of the other field. I don't know why there was not a lot of confusion, as most of the time, games WERE going on at both fields. Most of these games were for teams in the Industrial Leagues that were made up, I guess, mostly of teams from the various steel mills around town and the area.

Block Stadium

When you talk about Block Stadium, you are talking about what was, at the time, one of the premier high school baseball stadiums around—anywhere. The official name of the stadium complex is the 'E.J. Block Athletic Field". The stadium was built in 1942 by the Block family, the founders of Inland Steel. It had a capacity of about 3500. It was initially intended to be a place where the steelworkers and their families could go to play ball and relax. The stadium was donated to the City of East Chicago by the Blocks and was later used as the home field for the EC Washington Senators High School baseball team, and American Legion teams from around the region also played there. But really, when you talked about Block Stadium, you were referring to that whole Sports Complex of fields, which again, was way ahead of its time. The entire complex was bound on the North by 144th Street and stretched East to west from Elm Street to Parrish Avenue—about 4 city blocks, so it was pretty large. You had a soccer field out there, and about 3 practice baseball fields, but the center of attention for a lot of the young boys who grew up in The Harbor was the Little League Baseball Field. This field was The Bomb!

They had this concession stand and reporter's tower right behind home plate that overlooked the field. That's where the announcers sat upstairs, overlooking the action as they called the games. And then there was the field itself. It was truly the Field of Dreams for a lot of us kids that played ball there. We'd look forward to every summer, when you would have to try out for the Little League team of your choice, and after weeks of practice, if you were fortunate enough, you'd be handed your uniform and socks and cap right before the season started and you'd know you had made it! You didn't automatically make the team, but had to try out each year. There WAS a pretty good chance that if you had played on a team the prior year, you'd have a pretty good shot at making it again. Until age 12, when you'd have to move up to Senior League.

My team was Jarabak Drugs. That was our sponsor, Jarabak Drugstore, over on Columbus Drive. Chris Hernandez was our manager/coach. We had some pretty good players on the team—guys like Willie Campbell and Marcus Stallings and Eddie Foster and Petey Russell. These guys were all really good players and would usually make the all-star team every year. Petey was our star pitcher and I think Marcus pitched too. Willie was undoubtedly our best hitter and just about every time he came to bat, you expected a home run. Now me, I could barely hit the ball out of the infield, but my thing was 'The Crouch". Coach had taught us to crouch into a real compact size to decease the size of the strike zone to try and get some walks. Little League pitchers had not really pitched enough at that young age to have developed control yet, so that strategy worked really well. I got a lot of walks. And the thing was, if I got on first base with a walk, it was as good as a triple, because 9 times out of 10, I'd steal second base and then third base too!! Hitting might not have been my thing, but I could run. And on defense, I had nailed down the job as starting third baseman—The Hot Corner—because not too many balls got by me. All in all, I had a pretty nice Little League career. I finally made the all-star team in my last year in the league. I think that probably had a lot to do with the fact that our Jarabak Drugs team won the championship that year—in 1967—and so a lot of us got noticed more.

But, as I said, a LOT of boys that grew up in The Harbor played in that Little League system, and it kept us off the streets and gave us something to look forward to each summer. A lot of the guys moved on to play Senior League ball or in the Elks league, and quite a few even wound up playing for ECW when they got to High School. It was a great time to be a boy back then…

Chapter 11

The Tunnel and The Bridge

To those of us who grew up in The Harbor and went to Franklin Elementary School (or later, who were going to the Main Library), the prescribed route that most of us took to cross Columbus Drive led us through—The Tunnel... and later The Bridge (although the Bridge probably did not get built until around the time of Block Junior High. I never personally went on The Bridge. The first thing I personally think about when I think about The Tunnel is to an accident I saw right in front of it when I was a kid. I remember there was a person on a motorcycle and he got hit by a car. I remember seeing him go what seemed like, almost a mile into the sky, to a little kid. That is why I never got on a motorcycle to this very day!

But anyway, the point of this chapter is to provide memories of Harborites of The Tunnel and The Bridge. The smelly, dark, dank, foreboding, scary tunnel was the only way I used to get to Franklin from our home over on Fern Street when I attended Franklin during 2nd and 3rd grade. I guess it was about maybe a mile or a little over that from my house to the school, but sometimes that trip under Columbus Drive through the tunnel, seemed like the longest part of the trip.

The Tunnel and The Bridge

But let's just take a look at what some of the other kids who traversed that path had to say. Shall we???

> *Before the bridge was built there was a tunnel underneath Columbus Drive. It was dark, wet and smelled. I remember kids closing the doors on both ends while you were trying to cross. I remember kids crying and screaming and everyone running to get out.*
>
> *Riding your bike on the bridge was always an adventure. Making those tight turns and not crashing was always a challenge.*
>
> Anthony Mobley, May 22, 2008
1977 - 1981

> *Oh boy, do I remember that smelly, dark tunnel. Wow! I was so glad when that bridge was built, particularly because I didn't have to worry about crossing the street on a red light anymore and having my family laugh at me! Yep, they sure did. Ruined me for life. (LMAO). just kidding!*
>
> *The bridge was fun in the summer, but horrible in the winter.*
>
> Veda Johnson, May 22, 2008
1977—1979

> *The famous tunnel. A dark, wet, smelly hole. If you were lucky, occasionally you may encounter a mouse or rat running through. Thank God for a new way of passing over Columbus Drive.*
>
> *The new bridge is great for skate boarding without a board in the winter. (laugh). It's an obstacle course for other modes of transportation. Watch out for that sharp turn coming down.*
>
> Kim M. Mobley, May 30, 2008
1970—1974

I've had a few experiences with that bridge. We used to ride our bikes or push-cars down the long end of the bridge and try to make it to the bottom past that small S-Curve without using your brakes. There were some spectacular wipe-outs, and some of us made it through. I was fortunate. Whenever I'm in town, and I pass by that bridge, It has a special meaning to me and my brother Jermaine, who was also fortunate.

Gary Walton, May 28, 2008
1980 - 1985

I remember the tunnel. Dark and wet. The girls used to walk as fast as they can while holding down the back of our dresses. Every once in a while, someone would try to lift it. My scariest moment was when Kim Dent pushed me all the way home to our house on Butternut starting from the tunnel. Kim Dent, where are you????

Esperanza Mora Dennis, June 24, 2008
1973—1977

This was not funny at the time, but now it is. When the overpass was first built, I was skeptical about crossing because of my fear of heights. Well lo and behold, my first encounter... I held the handrails very, very tight and all was well. I was walking the incline, then it came time to cross the flat part, the part that crosses over Columbus Drive. I starting walking and then I froze. I could not move. My friends were trying to talk me through it. I believe it was Stephanie McGuire, Kathy Lewis and Melanese Johnson. With a little bit of prodding I finally made it across and the rest was easy, but I still had fear cause the next morning I would have to do it again.

Another funny story was my brother, Vincent, the adventurous one, riding his bike on it. I waited for him by the Credit Union, and when he came down he could not stop and crashed into the fence. He loved doing this and I don't know how many bikes he tore up, but he just would not stop.

Then I remember the TUNNEL. Dark, stinky, the steps were always sticky on your shoes, I could just imagine what all was and had been down there, it was just horrible. I remember how the "boys" would close the doors and we could not get out.

Those were the days, no troubles, no responsibilities, no ....., just us being kids and oblivious to all that was going on around us.

Vivian (Camille) Clayton, June 25, 2008
1973—1977

Yes, I do remember that bridge. I tell my stories of roller skating and bike riding to my kids. Boy, was that a lot of fun. One thing I used to hate about it was the winter time. Going down hill on either side when there was ice. My fear was that I would fall and be embarrassed, but luckily, if I remember, I never did fall. LOL

.I have a picture of my son on that bridge, but yet to take one of my daughter. She's getting older, so I better do it soon. Glad to see the bridge still standing tall!!

Alma Cappadora, August 10, 2008
1980 - 1984

Ahh....the famous bridge that everyone either seemed to run, ride a bike, skateboard or roller skate down!!! What fun we had! Oh but the INFAMOUS TUNNEL....Now that thing took courage....it was kind of like being half

scared and also half brave just to enter the thing! Geez...,I forgot about that tunnel - thanks for the memories!!!
Darcel Beaupain Resto, November 23, 2008
1965 - 1970

Wow! The nightmare tunnel. It's a comfort to know that I wasn't the only one terrified. The bridge was a relief. You know you're from the Harbor if you've experienced the tunnel, then the bridge, then you on your bike on the bridge, then you and your kids in strollers on the bridge and finally you and your kids on their bikes on the bridge. Wow, I'm old. Maybe I'll take my grand-daughter, yes, I said grand-daughter-shut up!- for a stroll on the bridge.
Sylvia M. Mora, September 5, 2008
1974 - 1978

What Was Going On

1980—1984

Year	Top Song Grammies - Record of the Year, Artist - R & B Song of the Year, Artist	
1980	What a Fool Believes	The Doobie Brothers
	After The Love Has Gone	Earth, Wind, and Fire
1981	Sailing	Christopher Cross
	Never Knew Love Like This Before	Stephanie Mills
1982	Bette Davis Eyes	Kim Carnes
	Just the Two of Us	Bill Withers
1983	Rosanna	Toto
	Turn Your Love Around	George Benson
1984	Beat It	Michael Jackson
	Billie Jean	Michael Jackson

Year	Oscar-Winning Movie	Other Movies
1980	Ordinary People	Raging Bull
1981	Chariots of Fire	Raiders of the Lost Ark
1982	Gandhi	An Officer and a Gentleman
1983	Terms of Endearment	Silkwood
1984	Amadeus	A Soldier's Story / Purple Rain

Year	TV Drama Emmy	TV Comedy Emmy
1980	Lou Grant	Taxi
1981	Hill Street Blues	Taxi
1982	Hill Street Blues	Barney Miller
1983	Hill Street Blues	Cheers
1984	Hill Street Blues	Cheers

Chapter 12

The Lake

The Lake (As I See It)

The Lake, it is so very big
The waves, they are so grey
It's a cool place to spend some extra time
On a Red-hot summer day

You can look as far as you can see
And You'll never see the end
You can enjoy its serenity by yourself
Or you can bring that Special Friend

You can sit upon the Sandy Beach
Or the huge, huge Rocks you'll find
You'll hear the sounds of Wave on Rock
Just let your Mind unwind

Yes, there's nothing that's quite like this Lake
No matter where you may roam
It's Magical, Mystical Memory
Will Always call you Home

I wrote that poem shortly after I got out of the Air Force and was sitting out at the Lake one day. The words just started coming and I was fortunate enough to see an old brown paper bag that I could write the words down on before I forgot them. For sure, there's nothing quite like…

The Lake, Lake Michigan, was also a big part of life in The Harbor. Besides being where the major job providers, Youngstown Sheet & Tube and Inland Steel were located, it was also the site of a lot of fun and recreation. Jeorse Park was located on the lakefront as was the marina where a lot of boats were docked. I never personally knew anyone that owned one of those fancy boats that were docked there, but there were sure a lot of them out there. And, just about any time you went out to the lake, you'd see somebody out there fishing. They might be 'smelting' or fishing for lake perch, or maybe even for the coho salmon that were supposed to be out there. And, as I got older, into my high school years, we used to ride out to the lakefront in our cars after stopping at the liquor store to see what kind of excitement we could find. I guess I was a little slow back then, because I never 'got busy' out at the lakefront. But judging from some of the posts that I will be sharing below, there were quite a few people who did!!! It was also out at the lakefront, while sitting on some of the huge rocks they have out there, that I wrote the poem, 'The Lake, (As I See It), which opened this chapter. **But anyway, since The Lake was such an integral part of life in The Harbor, let's look at it through the eyes of some of those who enjoyed it in various ways!**

Hey the lakefront was the spot until E.C.'s finest would come out and interrupt our groove. Some sitting outside, some sitting in the cars, some on the beach, some on the rocks, some on the grass, some leaving to make liquor runs, some cars rockin' with foggy windows and so on. Man! It was a beautiful thang. What was your experience at the Lakefront?

Charles Sanders, September 10, 2008
1982 - 1986

Oh man, the Lakefront, yeah! For the folks that worked at McDonald's, you know who you are! I hope I don't get in trouble for this, but we used to cook up some fresh burgers right before we closed. Then, we'd line an empty box with a clean plastic garbage bag. We'd put the fresh burgers and fries in there, seal it, then we put it in the garbage correl. Then, when the manager left, we circled back to pick up the grub and then we all headed to the Lakefront. Of course, we always had to make a stop to get some beverages before making it up there. It was nice watching the sun come up over the lake. We had lots of fun out there, Lots of lovin' going on. Lol

Anthony Puente, September 10, 2008
1982 - 1986

The lake front has ALWAYS been the spot. I remember going there with my family when I was a lil girl (after getting dairy queen). One of my first pics, is of my Dad holding me out @ the lake. It has always been a part of EC life. Then when I became a teenager we would go there to do everything LITERALLY under the Sun (moon) lol. Nowadays I still go there even though it's not the same. I always stay at one of the hotels right there on the lake when I come to visit.

Karen E. Covington, September 11, 2008
1982 - 1986

I remember hanging out there with the friends and I am glad (thank God) I got home in one piece. Denise, you know we liked the "beach" oh, the stories... :) You can tell Stephanie the time you came back from a "walk" with mud on your hands and dress... do you remember? Hahaha

Lenora Franco, September 11, 2008
1978 - 1982

Man you know the lake front was on. Chilling with family and friends, getting' bent or trying to get with the next girl that would give you the time of day or night. It was mellow most of the time, not a lot of drama. Don't know of too many places that still like that. I had several moments that I can remember. It was nice time n life.

Hosea Bridgeman, September 13, 2008
1984 - 1986

HUH!!!!!!!! The lakefront. Whenever my parents were not so strict and I could sneak out there with Karen, Tweety, Cookie, Kia, Raquel, Popa, Freeman, and you....... SQUID! Boy....that was fun. I only remember drinking a couple of sips of something and having to use the bathroom a lot!!!!!!!

Angelique M. Ard, September 23, 2008
1983 - 1986

Yes, the lakefront was one of the things in EC great for kids. It was a family gathering place on hot summer days and late at night the skinny dippers came out at the back

lake. This was the place to party! Of course I wasn't among the skinny dippers :) Those were the best days.
     Ceretha (Faye) Dukes-Howard, September 25, 2008
                   1962 - 1968

It was DEFINITELY the spot!!! I have many good memories, many bad memories, but mostly "fuzzy" memories... Different girls, different cars, different cliques...but it was all good. Never a dull moment...
       J.R. (Jake) Rodriguez, September 25, 2008
                   1979—1983

What memories. Oh my God. I met Jack Daniels there. I met Night Train there. I met Vodka there. Lucky I don't talk to Jack and I definitely don't get on any trains anymore, but vodka is my best friend. No, I'm not an alcoholic anymore lol. But the lakefront, it was the place to be. All the cool people hung out, made out, chilled out, and those who had to sneak out to be there including me. But I give a great big What Up to all those who attended faithfully. Sending out lots of love to 1987 Senators. Ok, maybe that was Cardinals, but I am a Senator at heart.
         Carmen Miranda, October 17, 2008
                   1983—1987

I remember the field trips across the prairie also. I also remember swimming at the pool at Washington Park and also at the lakefront. There used to be a concession stand at both and I had worked at both at one time. Music was always playing at both parks if I remember right. We even had a lifeguard at the lakefront.. .now you can't swim there. LOL. And Back Lake was the place for all the young lovers...hummm humm..
      Darcel (Beaupain) Resto, November 23, 2008
                   1965 - 1970

The Lake

Hmmm… Seems like there was a lot of lovin' and partyin' going on that I missed out on, out at The Lake ☺ !!! Oh well, I guess I couldn't do it all…

Chapter 13

Basketball Revisited

You can't talk about East Chicago, Indiana without talking about basketball. As any true sports fan knows, the state of Indiana is known for basketball and a thing called 'Hoosier Hysteria'. And folks up in the Northwest corner of the state, known as 'Da Region', are as crazy and fanatic, if not more, as those basketball fans in the rest of the state. 'Da Region' consists primarily of the Big Three cities of East Chicago, Gary, and Hammond, when it comes to basketball. There are a few other smaller cities around the region in Lake County, but those three are the only ones that matter, when it comes to talking High School Basketball and championships.

During the five years from 1968 to 1972, from when I was in 8th grade through my senior year, teams from 'Da Region' were in the Basketball Championship Game every year. In 1968, Gary Roosevelt won. In 1969, Gary Tolleston lost to a very talented Indianapolis Washington team. In 1970, the East Chicago Roosevelt Rough Riders won, going undefeated at 28-0. In 1971, my junior year, my school, the East Chicago Washington Senators, the greatest high school basketball team of all time, also went undefeated—at 29-0, 1 win better than Roosevelt. As a footnote, our game was the last championship basketball game played in Butler Fieldhouse in Indianapolis, after having been played there every year since 1946. And finally, in my senior year, Gary West Side High, lost in the title game. So you KNOW we were really going crazy with Hoosier Hysteria back during that period !!

But let's talk about High School Basketball in East Chicago. Through the end of the school year ending in 1986, there were two high schools in East Chicago—Washington (ECW) and Roosevelt (ECR). Attendance was basically determined by what side of town you lived in. If you lived west (I think) of the Viaduct on Columbus Drive in Nu-Addition, or in what was called East Chicago or in the Calumet section of town, you went to Roosevelt. If you lived in The Harbor, you went to Washington. Plain and Simple! To say that a bitter rivalry existed between the two schools in the athletic arena (especially in basketball) and in everyday life, was an understatement of the most profound proportions. We HATED those Roosevelt Rough Riders. If you were from The Harbor and ventured over to Calumet or Nu-Addition, you had better be prepared for a fight—unless you knew somebody over there who could vouch for you.

Now I may be a little (well, OK a LOT!) biased, but ECW was always the premier high school in the city, as far as I was concerned. We had the prettiest girls, the best athletes, the best basketball coach, the legendary Johnny Baratto, and of course, we had the Gym. Our gymnasium, where we played our home basketball games, held over 5000 people, and was one of the premier high school gyms in the state of Indiana, if not the whole United States at that time. You could walk through the halls surrounding the court downstairs, and see pictures of all the legendary players and teams that had graced those courts. Teams like the 1960 State Champions, with Trester Award Winner, Bobby Cantrell, and other photos of great players, like Bobby "Pop" Miles, among others. ECR played their home games on the stage of their auditorium!

The years 1970 and 1971 were very special years in the history of High School Basketball in East Chicago. In 1970, our arch-rivals, the East Chicago Roosevelt Rough Riders, won the state basketball championship with an undefeated 28-0 record. The next year, 1n 1971, we, the East Chicago Washington Senators, went them one better, winning the title with a perfect 29-0 record. It is believed that this is the only time that has ever happened in the history of high school basketball in this country—that is, having 2 different teams from the same city win back-to-back titles, with each going undefeated. So this was TRULY High times for Hoops in The Harbor !!!

Some of the players on those teams went on to have professional basketball careers in the NBA, like Jim Bradley of ECR, and Ulysses "Junior" Bridgeman of ECW. Timmy Stoddard of ECW went on to win an NCAA title as a basketball player with North Carolina State University and then had a long professional baseball career, winning a World Series Championship with the Baltimore Orioles. He and a later East Chicago product, Kenny Lofton, were the only two men ever to accomplish that particular double. And then we had Pete Trgovich, the scoring star on the ECW '71 title team. Turk went on to play for John Wooden at UCLA for 4 years, winning 2 NCAA titles, and then came full circle, coming back to coach the East Chicago Central (consolidation of ECW and ECR) Cardinals to the state championship in 2007. Darnell Adell went on to become the last basketball coach at ECW before they shut their doors and merged with

ECR to become the new East Chicago Central. He later became Principal of Central.

As you can imagine, 1971 was a wild ride on the journey to that championship. I can remember the wild bus trips we'd have as we partied down the road on our way to most of the road games that year to support the team. Trips to places like Kokomo and Terre Haute and Anderson. And then the Semi-State weekend in West Lafayette, before finally making it down to that big old barn called Butler Fieldhouse for the State Semi-Final and Final games. That was truly a season and time that will never be forgotten.

Here are a few remembrances from that season…

> *I remember the 1970-1971 school year when we were blessed enough to watch THE GREATEST HIGH SCHOOL BASKETBALL TEAM THAT EVER LACED THEM UP — Bar None!*

> *I remember some of those bus trips during the regular season to places like Terre Haute and Kokomo. I remember we were getting our 'drank' on, on the way to Kokomo while somebody had 'Psychedelic Shack' by The Tempts blasting on the radio And then gettin' our drank on some more at half-time under the bleachers at Kokomo. There was a lot more goin' on than just basketball that year. I also remember lockin' lips with one young lady for just about the whole bus ride back on one of those trips. She had the juiciest, sweetest lips I'd ever tasted - mmmm, mmmm, good!*

> *But our boys also shot some AWESOME hoop that year— as their 29-0 record (1 win more than ECR in their perfect year in 1970) attested to. We all remember the starters— Junior Bridge, Ruben and Darnell, Turk and Timmy*

Stoddard. But who else was on that team? Let's see... There was Satch, Tree, Paco, Marcus Stallings, Mike "Big Face" Monagan and I think Alex Kountoures and maybe Mike Muskin. Does that sound right?

Anyhow, who can forget Junior or Stoddard snagging a rebound and getting the ball downcourt to Ruben or Darnell for another of those lightning-fast fast breaks? Or Turk poppin' another "J" from the corner! What a season - What a Team !!!

Warren Landrum, November 24, 2008
1968—1972

I agree with all you said. Having lived in Indy for over twenty years, I'm tired of hearing about southern Indiana's {everything south of Da Region} basketball greatness. It was before my time, but Crispus Attucks teams with Oscar Robertson are the only ones I'd even allow discussion on. Lawrence North, Marion, Pike and all the others would have met the same fate as ECW's opponents that year. That was as complete a squad as I've ever seen and I've seen more basketball than most. Size, speed, great shooting and depth at EACH position. The non starters would have made a good team. While up tempo was our preference, that team was capable of any style. Even with all the illegal recruiting that goes on now, it is unlikely we'll see another team like that one anytime soon. Finding that much talent with the unselfishness of that group would be a formidable task for anyone. My thanks to that team and all the other great ones of ECW. The memories will last forever.

Winston Johnson, November 28, 2008
1973 - 1977

Basketball Revisited

The end result of the season: a State Championship.

A familiar sight: Pete Trgovich scores two points. Pete was the only unanimous selection to the All-State Team.

Varsity Record	ECW	OPP
Calumet	92	61
Crown Point	109	67
Hammond Gavit	95	43
Terre Haute Gerstmeyer	80	60
Gary Roosevelt	77	70
Whiting	100	58
Hammond Morton	73	50
Hammond Clark	92	51
Anderson	96	73
Holiday Tourney		
Munster	90	57
Warsaw	94	70
Laporte	91	50
Valparaiso	95	77
Kokomo	112	60
Hammond High	105	55
Hammond Tech	112	53
E.C. Roosevelt	89	50
Michigan City	110	89
Bishop Noll	106	73
Gary West Side	86	83

The things that made this year's Washington team great were teamwork and unselfishness of the individual players. The shooting and defense of All-Stater, Pete Trgovich, combined with the savage and efficient rebounding of Tim Stoddard and Howard Williams were only part of the total picture. Another portion of the picture centered around the steady scoring, consistent rebounding, and tight defensive work of Ulysses Bridgeman. The fast hands and feet of Ruben Bailey and Darnell Adell also provided a constant menace to the opposition in the form of blazing speed and ball thefts. The final slice of the picture centered around Albert Pollard and Francisco Sanchez, the back-up guards who always came through when needed. Put this together with speed, height, quickness, desire, and good coaching and you can have a good basketball team. Add team-work and unselfishness and you have the STATE CHAMPION WASHINGTON SENATORS!

Tournament Record	ECW	OPP
Sectional		
East Gary	71	39
E.C. Roosevelt	73	48
Hobart	87	56
Regional		
Hammond Clark	62	51
Gary West Side	94	89
Semi-State		
Michigan City	93	78
Rossville	76	67
State		
Floyd Central	102	88
Elkhart	70	60

What Was Going On

1985—1989

Year	Top Song Grammies - Record of the Year, Artist - R & B Song of the Year, Artist	
1985	What's Love Got to Do With It	Tina Turner
	I Feel For You	Prince
1986	We Are The World	USA For Africa
	Freeway of Love	Aretha Franklin
1987	Higher Love	Steve Winwood
	Sweet Love	Anita Baker
1988	Graceland	Paul Simon
	Lean on Me	Bill Withers
1989	Don't Worry, Be Happy	Bobby McFerrin
	Giving You the Best That I Got	Anita Baker

Year	Oscar-Winning Movie	Other Movies
1985	Out of Africa	The Color Purple
1986	Platoon	'Round Midnight
1987	The Last Emperor	Cry Freedom
1988	Rain Man	Mississippi Burning
1989	Driving Miss Daisy	Glory

Year	TV Drama Emmy	TV Comedy Emmy
1985	Cagney & Lacey	The Cosby Show
1986	Cagney & Lacey	The Golden Girls
1987	L.A. Law	The Golden Girls
1988	thirtysomething	The Wonder Years
1989	L.A. Law	Cheers

Chapter 14

The Last Chapter

This chapter has final remembrances that pretty much sum up what it was like growing up in The Harbor. Thanks to all my fellow Senators for their remembrances—especially to Larry Payne for the stirring opening reflections…

> *First, we survived being born to mothers who smoked and/or drank while they carried us.*
>
> *They took aspirin, ate blue cheese dressing, tuna from a can, and didn't get tested for diabetes.*
>
> *Then after that trauma, our baby cribs were covered with bright colored Lead-based paints.*
>
> *We had no childproof lids on medicine bottles, doors or cabinets and when we rode our bikes, we had no helmets, not to mention, the risks we took Hitchhiking.*
>
> *As children, we would ride in cars with no seat belts or air bags.*
>
> *Riding in the back of a pick up on a warm day was always a special treat.*
>
> *We drank water from the garden hose and NOT from a bottle.*

We shared one soft drink with four friends, from one bottle and NO ONE actually died from this.

We ate cupcakes, white bread and real butter and drank soda pop with sugar in it, but we weren't overweight because

WE WERE ALWAYS OUTSIDE PLAYING!

We would leave home in the morning and play all day, as long as we were back when the streetlights came on.

No one was able to reach us all day. And we were O.K.

We would spend hours building our go-carts out of scraps and then ride down the hill, only to find out we forgot the brakes. After running into the bushes a few times, we learned to solve the problem.

We played with mercury from broken thermometers, held it and we learned how neat a liquid metal was.

We did not have Playstations, Nintendo's, X-boxes, no video games at all, no 99 channels on cable, no video tape movies, no surround sound, no cell phones, no personal computers, no Internet or Internet chat rooms.........

WE HAD FRIENDS and we went outside and found them!

We fell out of trees, got cut, broke bones and teeth and there were no lawsuits from these accidents.

We ate worms and mud pies made from dirt, and the worms did not live in us forever.

We were given BB guns for our 10th birthdays, made up games with sticks and tennis balls and although we were told it would happen, we did not put out very many eyes.

We rode bikes or walked to a friend's house and knocked on the door or rang the bell, or just walked in and talked to them!

Little League had tryouts and not everyone made the team. Those who didn't had to learn to deal with disappointment. Imagine that!!

The idea of a parent bailing us out if we broke the law was unheard of. They actually sided with the law!

This generation has produced some of the best risk-takers, problem solvers and inventors ever!

The past 50 years have been an explosion of innovation and new ideas.

We had freedom, failure, success and responsibility, and we learned

HOW TO DEAL WITH IT ALL!

And YOU are one of them! CONGRATULATIONS!
Larry Payne, August 2, 2008
1963 - 1967

How true this is!!! What memories! Our children today do not appreciate enough. There is one other one that I remember that is not on your list. This one is true for all the girl's (women) out there: Remember when we use to use baby oil to get the best sun tan just in time to go to all the parties! They never warned us about skin cancer back then.
Elizabeth Becerra Cantu, August 7th
1983 - 1985

That was so thought provoking and true! Especially the part about leaving home to go play and being out all day long, as long as you made it in before the street lights came on. No wonder we were always eating at each others houses, because you ate when your friends did, or vice versa. My brothers were all over the Harbor playing more so than my sister and me. But there was no worries of anyone doing them any harm, except an occasional fight. And being out all day made for so many "adventures" that we still laugh about. The mud pies seemed real, especially after decorating them with rocks, grass and sand. Anyone remember hopscotch? One thing about it, if you made it in the Harbor, you could make it anywhere, and the lives on this website prove it. The Harbor bred good stock.

Diane Jones Dillard, August 18, 2008
1959 - 1965

Hi Larry. I don't know who u are….But what can I say…. that u haven't already said…….Those were the good old days………Santa…….

Santa, September 5, 2008
1969 - 1971

Epilogue

Well, that's pretty much it. I've got one 'Bonus Chapter' that I'm inserting after this, but for the most part, we're all done.

Did this book help to take you back in time, stirring up some of those lost or long-forgotten, buried memories about 'The Good Old Days'? I hope it did. Plain and simple, that's all I wanted to do. We've got enough to worry about with all the problems and things we have to deal with in our everyday lives and in the 'Real World'. So I just wanted to give you a break, and take you back to yesteryear. If you got a good chuckle or were able to do some 'time-travelling' back to those days of yore, feel free to give me a holler at my e-mail address and let me know what you think or how you felt afterwards. I'd love to know.

                Cheers,

                Warren G. Landrum, Jr.
                Aka 'Champ'
                Class of '72
                warrenglandrum@hotmail.com

Bonus Chapter

This chapter is being included in the book, mainly because I think it's a good little story and I wanted to publish it somewhere. And this is as good a place as any. While it may not be representative of the way ALL kids grew up in The Harbor, I'm sure some readers will be able to relate or it will take them to a similar place all their own. At least, I hope it does.

So come on, and go with me on….

The Midnight Fishing Trip

When he came into my bedroom to wake me and tell it was time to go, I was already ready! Although I was only about 9 years old, I had been on enough of these 'midnight fishing trips' to know what to do. It was about 11:30pm and I popped out of bed fully clothed, with a grin on my face that stretched from ear to ear. My Dad started laughing, because we'd replayed this scenario many times already in my young life.

"I should have known by now you'd be ready to go! Go get our lunch out the 'frigerator and start taking it to the car."

I joyfully ran into the kitchen, opened the fridge, and saw the brown bags he'd already packed with food. That's one of the main things I liked about these trips. We could eat all kinds of what I thought of as 'Man Food'. Now don't get me wrong. I loved my mother's cooking, and I thought she was the best cook on the planet!. But the food we ate on these fishing trips just seemed like it was more fun to eat. I peeked into the bags and all the old staples were there. There were the ham and cheese sandwiches slathered with Hellman's Real Mayonnaise, 4 dark purple, juicy plums, a couple tins of sardines and Vienna sausages and some crackers to go with them, 4 hard-boiled eggs (with salt wrapped in aluminum foil), a couple Snickers bars, and 4 cans of pop. What a feast! I don't know if I liked these trips more for the fishing or for the food. But I think the main thing I liked about them was that it gave me a chance to have some alone time with my Dad. No bratty little sister. No brother. No Mom, reminding me to take out the garbage—just me and him!

And I know that Dad really enjoyed these trips, as well. He would always talk about what a pleasure it was to get away from the daily toils grinding it out at #2 Tin Mill at Youngstown Sheet & Tube Company in his role as a steelworker. He said after being in that hot, noisy, dangerous place day in and day out, he couldn't WAIT to get out on the lake and drop a line in the water!

We got all the fishing gear and food loaded up and hopped into the car for our hour-long drive to the lake. The reason we left around midnight was because we were going fishing for Bullheads and Bluegills. And everybody knows that Bullheads usually start biting around 1 or 2am and Bluegills started going crazy right before daybreak. At least that's what Dad told me, and he was NEVER wrong when it came to fishing!

Bonus Chapter

After we turned off the Interstate and went a few miles and turned onto the dirt road that would take us to the lake, I turned to Dad and asked, "Think we'll catch anything tonight?"

"We'll get 'em," he said confidently. "There's a south wind and we got almost a full moon."

I nodded and grinned, satisfied that our venture would be successful.

We got to the place where they had the little rowboats lined up and parked the car as close as we could to the water. There were three rowboats left. We started inspecting each one to make sure we got a good one. There was a big light pole on the dock overlooking the boats, so that made it easy to see. We settled on one that seemed the driest, had a couple good anchors, and two solid oars. Back in those days, the honor system was in effect, so all you had to do was pick a boat, and just pay for it whenever you got back in the next day..

So we loaded all of our gear—and the food—into the boat and set out to go get 'em! The rowboat had three rows of seats, so I sat in the front row near the pointed vee, and Dad sat in the back row. We sat like that to balance the boat. I pulled the front anchor up and Dad untied the boat from the dock, sat down, grabbed the oars, and started rowing, and we were off!

It seemed like we were just gliding or floating along the water. It was so peaceful, with the moonlight shining down on us and reflecting in the water. My dad was such a good rower that the paddles hardly made any sound when they pushed the water back and the boat forward. Likewise, the boat barely disturbed the water. I sat with my back to the front, facing my dad. His face looked so peaceful and serene, and yet, so strong and determined. I don't think, before or since that time, that I have ever had such a feeling. It was like 'All is right with the World. The Universe is in balance and everything is as it should be'.

"Well, I think this looks like a pretty good place to start," Dad said, interrupting my thoughts. "Go 'head and drop your anchor, and I'll drop mine, and let's go get 'em!" I could hear the excitement in his voice. It was as though he were a kid again himself.

It didn't take long—maybe five minutes or so—before I got my first nibble.

"Dollar on the first fish," I slyly said, knowing he hadn't seen my bite yet.

"Bet," he said.

My fish bit again, I set the hook—and missed. Darn! Within another 5 minutes, Dad had the first fish of the night in the boat and said, "You owe me a dollar," and started laughing.

After about an hour or so, when I had landed only 2 Bullheads, while watching him pull in around 9 or 10, I sat down in the bottom of the boat, and started digging through our lunch. I started munching on a ham sandwich, and opened a can of grape pop. The action had kind of slowed down at Dad's end of the boat, too, so he told me to toss him some sardines and crackers. I did, and he started munching away. So there we were—Two Landrum Fishermen—on top of the world!

It was at around that point that I asked him a question and I think the answer he gave was probably the most revealing moment of his life, to me. I asked,

"Dad, if you could be anything in the world that you wanted to be, what would you be?"

He paused and thought for a moment, and answered, "You know, I'd probably be a carpenter. I really enjoy working with my hands and building things."

That's it. There it was. The moment quickly passed, but I've never forgotten it. And as I look back over the years and think about some of the projects we did together, like lowering the ceiling in our living room, dining room and kitchen or measuring for, cutting and laying the carpet in our house, I can remember how he really did seem to be at peace and in total control.

But anyway, almost as soon as those words were out of his mouth, I saw his rod bend over and start whipping up and down. I yelled, "Dad, you got a bite, you got a bite!" He swallowed that piece of sardine, and in one motion, swung effortlessly around to his rod, and the next time it bent, he set the hook—and got 'im !

In Conclusion

As the author, my purpose for this book is to share with the reader my reflections and memories and those of others who went to the same high school—East Chicago Washington High, in East Chicago, Indiana.

This book does NOT attempt to be a documentary of the era (1960's—1980's) that it covers. There WERE other things going on in East Chicago at that time, as there were in all cities—things in the areas of politics, crime, drugs and such; but that is not the focus of this book.

It is the hope of the author that these shared memories and reflections will trigger similar happy memories in the reader. If you, the reader, also come away with some idea of what it was like to grow up in a multicultural community that was a true microcosm of the bigger melting pot that is America, then that's a good thing, and a bonus.

I hope you enjoyed your trip down Memory Lane !!!

—Warren

Appendix A

The following is a list of some famous East Chicagoans and their claim to fame.

- Wendell Campbell, Architect
- Greg Popovich, NBA Coach, San Antonio Spurs
- Tim Stoddard, Retired MLB Pitcher
- Frank Reynolds, ABC TV Anchor
- Steve Tesich, Oscar winning Screenwriter
- Betsy Palmer, Actress
- Kenny Lofton, MLB Star
- Emilio A. De La Garza, USMC Medal of Honor Recipient
- Angel Manfredy, Junior Welterweight Boxer
- Jr. Bridgeman, Retired NBA Basketball Star Owner of Bridgeman Foods, one of the largest Wendy's franchises in the U.S.

Appendix B

Contributor	Years Attended	Chapter(s)
Richard Amescua	84-86	9
Angelique M. Ard	83-86	12
Kim S. Askew	84-86	3
Frankie Askew Banks	63-69	3
Hosea Bridgeman	84-86	12
Conception (Flores) Bueno	62-65	7
Roshanta Buggs	84-86	3
Elizabeth Becerra Cantu	83-85	14
Alma Cappadora	80-84	11
Diane Casas	80-84	7
Azalia 'Sally" Castro	74-78	7
Vivian (Camille) Clayton	73-77	11
Nettie Person Collins	63-68	3
Karen E. Covington	82-86	12
Carmen Cruz	67-71	7
Greg "Chico" Davis	69-73	4,7
Esperanza Mora Dennis	73-77	11
Diane Jones Dillard	59-65	3,14
Francisca Flores Duenas	77-81	9
Ceretha (Faye) Dukes-Howard	62-68	4,12
Tyna L. Findley (Joshua)	82-86	4
Lenora Franco	78-82	7,12
Helen Smith Flynn	56-61	3,7

Appendix A

William "Joey" France	64-70	7
Gerardo Gaitan	72-76	7
Karen Lynn George-Dates	74-78	3
Debra Darcel Gil	66-69	4,9
Marc Glick	74-78	4
Aniba "Nebo" Gonzalez	81-85	7
Vilma Gonzalez	77-81	7
Magaly Gonzalez-Williams	84-86	3
Elozia Ann Jernigan-Neeley	64-69	3,7
Jeanette Johnson Jackson	61-68	9,10
Janice Johnson	66-71	7
Veda Johnson	77-79	4,11
Winston Johnson	73-77	7,10,13
Sandra Kemp	72-75	3
Sherry Shapiro Kessel	62-67	10
Warren G. Landrum, Jr.	68-72	4,7,13
Anthony Lang	72-75	7
Lisa Lang	73-77	10
Terilyn Lloyd	80-81	3
Carlos Longoria	65-68	7
Lisa Minjarez	83-86	7
Carmen Miranda	83-86	12
Anthony Mobley	77-81	4,11
Christopher Mobley	74-78	4
Kim M. Mobley	70-74	11
Joel Moore	76-79	4
Sylvia M. Mora	74-78	11
Baron Moss	83-86	3
Annette (Sessions) Ortega	74-77	7
Larry Payne	63-67	7,10,14
James Merrill Pearcey	63-68	4
Ursula Pepper	84-86	4
Maria E. Porras	82-85	7

Anthony Puente	79-83	4,13
Elizabeth Santos Quinones	79-83	4,9
Belinda Rangel	78-82	9
Darcel (Beaupain) Resto	65-70	10,11,12
Jenny Rodriguez	74-78	7
J.R. (Jake) Rodriguez	79-83	12
Paree Roper	72-76	4
Dorothy Marajanovich Rybicki	65-69	7
Charles Sanders	82-86	7,12
Santa	69-71	14
Jacqueline Smith	79-83	7
Lynn Threatt	79-83	3
Damaris Torres	74-78	9
Gwendolyn (Aikens) Upshaw	81-85	7
Toni Walker	69-73	3
Gary Walton	80-85	11

References

A Rich History. (n.d.). Retrieved December 1, 2008 from East Chicago Public Library website: www.ecpl.org/History/history.asp

Davis, K. (2008). *EC Washington online, Before we became legends, we were SENATORS!!!* http://ecwonline.ning.com

About the Author...

Warren G. Landrum, Jr. was born in East Chicago, Indiana on October 11, 1954. He grew up and was raised there until he went off to college to Purdue University, from which he graduated with a degree in Information Systems and Computer Programming.

Warren is also a member of Alpha Phi Alpha Fraternity, Inc., the first Black Greek-Letter Fraternity, established in 1906.

Warren served in the U.S. Air Force, both at home and abroad. It was while in the Air Force that he first became exposed to overseas travel, a passion that he would pursue at every opportunity throughout his life. While stationed in Germany, he was able to travel throughout Europe, experiencing the various cultures and lifestyles in Holland, Switzerland, France, Luxembourg, Belgium, and Great Britain.

Warren continued his traveling ways upon entering corporate America. He had remote assignments in Bermuda

(7 months), Taiwan, Bangkok, Thailand (12 trips); and back to Europe again, this time experiencing Paris, Milan, Munich, and the London-Reading area. All of those experiences, along with his leisure/vacation travel to various parts of Mexico, Canada, The Bahamas, Jamaica and throughout the US, along with being married to a Jamaican wife, have truly given Warren a global perspective and insight in regards to both observing life and living life !!

In addition to traveling, Warren's other passions are fishing, which he inherited as part of the Landrum gene-pool/DNA, basketball, and performing as a singer. He has performed in some capacity as either a secular or gospel singer from his elementary school years and throughout his adult life. He founded the Sun Valley Revue, a sextet of talented singer/entertainers who performed 'old-school' R&B music for around two years in the Phoenix, Arizona area in the late 1990's. Warren's most recent musical endeavor was as Director of the Male Chorus at Tanner Chapel AME Church in Phoenix.

Warren G. Landrum, Jr. began to write poetry about his life and loves while stationed in Germany. During his stint in the Air Force he became exposed to overseas travel, a passion that he would pursue at every opportunity throughout his life.

Warren and his beautiful wife Carol are the parents of one daughter, Suzette.

For further information about this book or for appearances, you can reach Warren Landrum at 214-538-2287 or email him at: warrenglandum@hotmail.com.

ORDER FORM

Please Mail Checks or Money Orders to:

Warland Books
2791 Explorador
Grand Prairie, TX 75054

Warrenglandrum@hotmail.com
Phone: 214-535-2287

Please send ___ copy(ies) of
Let's Go Home To Indiana Harbor

Name: _____

Address: _____

City: _____ State: ____ Zip: _____

Telephone: (____)_____ / (____)_____

Email: _____

I have enclosed $10.95, plus $5.00 shipping per book for a total of $_____.

Sales Tax: Add 8.25% to total cost of books for orders shipped to TX addresses.

For Bulk or Wholesale Rates, Call: 214-536-2287

www.ingramcontent.com/pod-product-compliance
Lightning Source LLC
Chambersburg PA
CBHW072051290426
44110CB00014B/1644